A Gentle Introduction to Agile a
by Stephen Haunts

Published by Stephen Haunts Ltd

www.stephenhaunts.com

Cover by Zeljka Kojic

Table of Contents

About the Author...10

Agile Software Introduction...13

Who Is This Book For?...13

Waterfall Development and it's Problems...............................14

History of the Waterfall Model..14

How Does Waterfall Work? 15

Where Is Waterfall Suitable? 17

Advantages and Disadvantages of Waterfall 19

History of the V-Model 23

How Does the V-Model Work? 23

Where Is the V-Model Suitable?...26

Advantages and Disadvantages of the V-Model...................27

Agile Software Development 29

What Is Agile? 29

A Brief History of Agile...31

The Agile Manifesto 4 Core Values 31

Agile Methodology Overview 33

Roles within an Agile Team..37

Common Agile Misconceptions 39

Agile Misconceptions...39

Advantages and Disadvantages 45

Advantages of Agile 45

Disadvantages of Agile...50

What Are Your Department's Biggest Challenges?................51

Are You Prepared for Agile? 53

Extreme Programming (XP) 55

History of Extreme Programming 55

Overview of Extreme Programming.......................57

Activities 57

Values 60

Principles...62

Practices..64

Rules 69

Extreme Programming Diagram 81

Scrum..83

Definition and History of Scrum..........................83

Overview of Scrum..85

Visualizing Scrum 88

Scrum Roles 89

Scrum Ceremonies..93

Scrum Artifacts..95

Extreme Programming vs. Scrum...........................99

Lean Software Introduction 102

Our Fictional Company 104

Lean Manufacturing...105

History of Lean Manufacturing 105

Henry Ford and the Model-T 105

The Toyota Production System 107

Automation..108

Types of Waste 108

Lean Principles 110

Kaizen - Continuous Improvement 111

Plan, Do, Check, Act 112

5 Why's 112

Lean Software Development 114

The Origins of Lean Software Development 115

Lean Software Development Principles 116

Eliminate waste.. 116

Eliminate Waste - Value Stream Maps 121

Build quality/integrity in 124

Amplifying learning... 125

Feedback.. 126

Iterations.. 127

Decide as late as possible 127

Deliver as fast as possible 128

Empowering the team 129

Seeing the whole 133

Applying Lean Software Development 135

Eliminate Waste - The 7 Wastes 136

Defects 136

Extra Features 139

Handoffs.. 140

Delays.. 140

Partially Completed Work... 141

Task Switching... 142

Unneeded Processes...143

Eliminate Waste - Value Stream Mapping 145

Amplify learning..149

Feedback...149

Iterations..150

Knowledge sharing..151

Code reviewing 151

Build integrity in..152

Decide as late as possible 154

Deliver as fast as possible 155

Empower the team 155

Seeing the whole 156

Agile vs Lean 159

Agile Benefits 159

Lean Benefits 164

Agile vs Lean 165

Software Practices to Support Lean...................................167

Source Control Management...168

Centralized Source Control 169

Distributed Source Control 171

Continuous Integration and Delivery..............................175

Developers and the CI Process.....................................177

Automated Testing and TDD..181

Unit Testing..181

Kanban 187

Kanban Background 187

Work in Progress 188

Planning, Cycle Time, and Focus 192

    Minimizing cycle time 192

    Scrum vs Kanban 193

Summary 196

*This book is dedicated to my wife Amanda and my kids,
Amy and Daniel, who are always putting up with my
personal projects.*

Thank you for purchasing, A Gentle Introduction to Agile and Lean Software Development. If you like this book, I would be very grateful for you leaving a review on Amazon. I read all reviews and will try to address any constructive feedback with updates to the book. You can review the book in your country at the following links, or from your local Amazon website.

Amazon.com

Amazon.co.uk

Amazon.de

Amazon.fr

If you enjoyed this book, you might like other books I have in the "Gentle Introduction To" series. I have written these short guides to focus on specific niches and make them brief enough to read in a short space of time, but also detailed enough that they offer a lot of value.

If you wish to see what other high-value books I have in this series, then please visit my web page at the following link.

https://stephenhaunts.com/books/

About the Author

Stephen Haunts has been developing software and applications professionally since 1996 and as a hobby since he was 10. Stephen has worked in many different industries including computer games, online banking, retail finance, healthcare, and pharmaceuticals. Stephen started out programming in BASIC on machines such as the Dragon 32, Vic 20 and the Amiga and moved onto C and C++ on the IBM PC. Stephen has been developing software in C# and the .NET framework since first being introduced to it in 2003.

As well as being an accomplished software developer, Stephen is also an experienced development leader and has led, mentored and coached teams to deliver many high-value, high-impact solutions in finance and healthcare.

Outside of Stephen's day job, he is also an experienced tech blogger who runs a popular blog called Coding in the Trenches at www.stephenhaunts.com, and he is also a training course author for the popular online training company Pluralsight. Stephen also runs several open source projects including SafePad, Text Shredder, Block Encrpytor, and Smoke Tester—the post deployment testing tool.

Stephen is also an accomplished electronic musician and sound designer.

Agile
Software
Development

Agile Software Introduction

Who Is This Book For?

This book will appeal to many different audiences. If you are a developer, then this book will give you a good understanding of why Agile is beneficial to you, your team, and your employer. This might be the first agile project that you've worked on, and you want to understand why you're using Agile over Waterfall. This book will also be an excellent refresher on why you're using Agile if you're already on an agile project.

If you're a project manager, then this book will help you understand the difference between an agile project and the more traditional Waterfall project. As teams become more self-directed when working on a project, a project manager is still crucial to help ensure the teams are operating correctly and that the team delivers on time and budget.

If you're an IT or business leader and your company is considering adopting Agile, this book will also help you understand how this will work and what the benefits are to your organization. This book is split down into six main areas.

- Waterfall development and its problems,

- What is agile all about?

- Typical Agile misconceptions,

- Advantages and Disadvantages

- Extreme Programming (XP)

- Scrum

Waterfall Development and it's Problems

History of the Waterfall Model

The Waterfall development methodology was introduced by the computer scientist Winston Royce in 1970. Winston Royce first discussed the ideas of Waterfall software development in an article called Managing the Development of Large Software Systems. Winston Royce didn't refer directly to the model in his paper as Waterfall development. This article was about a process that was flawed for software development. Royce's original design actually allowed for more repetition between stages of the model which Waterfall doesn't let you do.

Winston Royce's actual model was more iterative in how it worked and allowed more room to maneuver between stages. We will discuss a more frequentative way of working when we discuss Agile later on in this book. Although Royce didn't refer to this model as the Waterfall mode directly, he is credited with the first description of what we refer to as the waterfall model.

Royce's original article consists of the following stages, which we'll go into more detail on in a moment. Those stages are the

- Requirements Specification stage
- Detail Design stage
- Construction phase
- Integration
- Testing and Debugging
- Installation, Maintenance

How Does Waterfall Work?

In Waterfall, the process is divided into separate stages, where the outcome of one stage is the input of the next stage. The first stage in a Waterfall will start with the Requirements covering all requirements analysis, where all of the requirements for the system being developed are recorded in a specification document. This requirements specification will then need to be signed off by another project stakeholder, usually from the business.

It is the responsibility of the business analyst on the project to create the requirements document, but if you are working on a smaller team, then it could be done as a collaboration between team members. In this stage of the waterfall cycle, the business analyst, or persons writing the document try to capture all the requirements and features of the system from the key business stakeholders. This could include the complete set of functionalities, any business rules that need automating, and any other operational processes from a company and regulatory perspective.

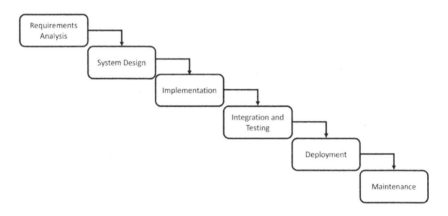

The waterfall software development process

The next stage is System Design. The Requirement specifications from the first stage are inspected, and the system design is put together. This design helps in specifying the design requirements, and also helps with creating the overall systems architecture. In this stage, it is the technical members of the team, which includes developers and architects that decide how the overall system will be built.

Once the system design phase is complete, we move into the implementation phase. This is where the developers on the team take the previous software design and start writing the code to make it work.

After the implementation phase, we then move into the integration and testing phase. This is where a testing team will bring all the system components together and test them as a single product. The test team at this stage should have a detailed testing plan that they work towards by either performing manual testing or developing automated tests. Once the testing team has completed its work and signed off the system as fit and proper, it is then ready for deployment to the end users who can start seeing the benefits.

Once the solution has been deployed into production, it will then go into a maintenance phase. During this period, if the end users report any defects, they will get fixed, tested and then redeployed into production.

If any of these fixes end up being very large in scope, then the decision might be made to start the waterfall again by redefining the requirements, designing, implementing, testing and deploying. If this happens though, it can be quite time-consuming, which wouldn't lend itself to fixes that have to be made in urgency.

Where Is Waterfall Suitable?

While in the agile world, there is a lot of emphasis on saying that waterfall is not suitable, there are some software projects where the Waterfall methodology is appropriate. Let's take a look at a few.

First, Waterfall is suitable if your software projects requirements are already well defined and documented, but how often is that the case though? From my own experiences as a software designer and developer, I can't remember any of the many projects I've delivered where the requirements have been clear from the start so that they can be captured in a document that doesn't change as the project rolls on.

Next, the product definition must be stable. Again, I can't think of a single project where this has been the case, as external factors like a change in the marketplace or a shift in business priorities mean that your product will evolve. I have worked on many projects where the final delivered product was entirely different from what was initially specified. Under Waterfall, this shouldn't happen, but in reality, what you are building can change. There is nothing wrong with this, but it does fight against software delivery process.

Next, the technology should be well understood. This means that developers should understand the technologies that they're going to be using and how they work. Once you enter the implementation and construction phase of the project, developers usually have to work toward very rigid and set timescales. In my experience working on a Waterfall project, a lot of effort is expelled on the requirements and design phases, which normally eat into the time needed actually to develop the code.

Next, Waterfall works best on projects that are short, and by short, I mean projects that are around 2-4 months in total. The longer a project runs for, the more chance there is that the requirements and product definition are becoming out of date.

Finally, Waterfall works best when all of your product team are available to work together. It is quite normal for a development team to have a pool of resources that might be shared out between many different projects. If another project is over-run for any reason, you may not have all your people available at the time when they are required. This can significantly impact a project's timescale and put delivery dates at risk.

Advantages and Disadvantages of Waterfall

In a moment, we'll take a look at some pros and cons of the Waterfall model. But before we do, I first want to cover some of the main high-level advantages and disadvantages to this development process.

The first advantage is that by splitting your project deliveries into different stages, it is easier for an organization to maintain control over the development process. This makes it much easier for schedules to be planned out in advance. This makes a project manager's life much more comfortable. It's for this reason I've found that experienced project managers tend to favor the Waterfall process as it can make their lives much easier. By splitting a project down into the various phases of the Waterfall process, you can easily departmentalize the delivery of your project, meaning that you can assign different roles to various departments and give them a clear list of deliverables and timescales. If any of these departments can't deliver on time for various reasons, it is easier for a project manager to adjust their overall plan.

Unfortunately, in reality, I've seen the method adapted where the implementation phase gets squeezed more and more, which means the development team has less time to deliver a working solution, and this can mean quality suffers and shortcuts tend to be taken. It's usually code-base unit and integration testing that gets affected first. This has a knock effect that the testing teams in the test phase get a solution that contains more problems, which makes their lives very hard. So, while departmentalization is seen as an advantage, it can quickly become a disadvantage if another team is late delivering their part of the project.

Now let's take a look at some of the high-level disadvantages. The Waterfall model doesn't allow any time for reflection or revision to a design. Once the requirements are signed off, they're not supposed to change. This should mean that the development team has a fixed design that they're going to work towards. In reality, this does not happen, and changes in requirements can often result in chaos as the design documents need updating and re-signing off by stakeholders.

By the time the development team starts their work, they are pretty much expected to get it right the first time, and they're not allowed much time to pause for flaws and reflection on the code that they have implemented. By the time you get to the point where you think a change of technical direction is required, it is usually too late to do anything about it unless you want to affect the delivery dates. This can be quite de-motivating for a development team, as they have to proceed with technical implementations that are full of compromises and technical debts. Once a product has entered the testing stage, change is virtually impossible, whether that is to the overall design or the actual implementation.

Now we've seen some of the high-level advantages and disadvantages. Let's take a more in-depth look at more of the benefits of the Waterfall model. The waterfall is a simple process to understand, and on paper, it seems like a good idea for running a project. The waterfall is also easier to manage for a project manager as everything is delivered in stages that can be scheduled and planned. Phases are completed one at a time where the output from one phase is fed into the input of the next stage. Waterfall works well for smaller projects where the risk of changing requirements and scope is lower. Each step in Waterfall is very clearly defined. This makes it easier to assign clear roles to teams and departments who have to feed into the project. Because each stage is well defined, it makes a milestone set up by the project manager easier to understand. If you're working on a stage like Requirements Analysis, you should know what you need to deliver to the next phase, and by when.

Under Waterfall, the process and results of each stage are well documented. Each stage has clear deliverables that are documented and signed off by key project stakeholders. The Waterfall model fits very neatly into a Gant chart, so a project manager is happier when they can plan everything out and view a project timeline in an application like Microsoft Project.

The biggest disadvantage of the Waterfall model is you don't get any working software until late in the process. This means that your end users don't get to see their vision come to life until it is too late to change anything. It can be tough for non-technical people to be clear about how they want an application to operate, and it isn't normally until they can visualize an application that they can give good feedback. You can mitigate this a bit by doing some prototyping in the system design phase to help users visualize their system, but there is nothing like giving them the actual working code to try out.

The Waterfall model can introduce a high level of risk and uncertainty for anything but a small project. Just because a set of requirements and design has been signed off, does not mean that the conditions won't change. The Waterfall is all about getting the requirements, design, and implementation right the first time, which is a grand idea in a perfect world, but in the real world it is very rarely the case, and this is a big risk to a project. The more complexity that is involved increases the risk of the change needed further down the line. Complexity in the system is also very hard to implement and test, and can often cause delays in the later stages of the Waterfall software development lifecycle.

If you're working on a project where change is expected, then Waterfall is not the right model for you. I've worked on projects for a financial services company, where variations in financial law were causing compliance regulations to change. Unfortunately, these rules are very open to interpretation, which meant the legal team was involved at a very early stage. This meant that the interpretation changed a few times during the project. If this had been a Waterfall project, we would have been in big trouble, as projects frequently come with a sturdy and fixed set of deadlines.

This was a perfect fit for an agile project. If you are working on a large project and the scope changes, the impact of this can be so expensive and costly, that the original business benefit for the project can evaporate and then the project is canceled. I've seen this happen a couple of times, and it's a real shame, as projects that show real promise are stopped due to restrictions in the process.

Finally, the integration and delivery of a project are done as a "Big Bang" on a Waterfall project. This means you're introducing massive amounts of change all at once. This can quickly overwhelm testing teams and your operational teams.

History of the V-Model

Now that we've finished taking a look at the traditional Waterfall model let's take a look at a model that builds on Waterfall. This is called the V-Model. As opposed to the Waterfall method, the V-Model was not designed to run in a linear fashion. Instead, the process is turned upwards after the implementation or coding stage is complete which makes the V shape. The V-Model is based on the idea of having a testing stage for each development stage. This means that for every single stage in the development cycle there is a directly associated testing phase. This is a strict model, and the next step starts only after the completion of the previous stage. Now let's take a look at how the V-Model works.

How Does the V-Model Work?

With the V-Model, the detailed testing of the development stage is planned in parallel, so there are verification steps on one side of the V and the validation stages on the other side. The coding and implementation phases join both sides of a V-Model together.

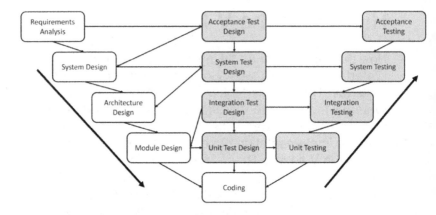

The V-Model software development process

When you draw out the V-Model, it can look a bit complicated, but once you break it down, it's quite straightforward. First is the Requirements Analysis phase. This is the first phase of the product development process where the customer requirements are understood which requires collaboration with the client to understand his/her expectations. As most clients are not entirely sure about what they need, the Acceptance Test Design planning is completed at this stage as any business requirements can be used as input for the acceptance testing.

Next is System Design. Once you understand the requirements, you put together a complete design of the entire system. This design will include both software and hardware/infrastructure design. At the same time as preparing the system design, you would usually put the system test design together too so that your test teams can pre-plan their testing activities.

Then we have the Architectural Design. The architectural design will look at a much broader design focus than the system design. This may even result in multiple designs being proposed that balance vendors, costs, and other factors.

Unit-tests are a critical piece of any development process and help identify bugs in the code early so that the team has early visibility of any breakages caused by other dependencies. Once all of these design phases are completed, you can then proceed to the coding stage. The language used in the coding stage along with the architecture should already have been agreed upon by this point, allowing developers to make an immediate start.

Next, we enter the validation phase of the V-Model. First, we have unit testing. Unit tests designed in the Module Design stage are run against the code during its validation stage. Unit testing is a test at the code level and helps eliminate bugs at an early stage, although all defects cannot be uncovered by unit testing alone, they do give a good indication quickly as to any breakages that may or may not occur. This does mean that the developers have to be quite disciplined in writing good unit tests that add value and don't just check language features. Following on we have the Integration Testing phase. Integration tests are performed to check the co-existing of different modules or components within the system; here we are making sure that all integration between various components within the system as a whole is working as expected.

After integration testing, we have system testing. System tests check the entire systems functionality and the communication between all other external systems. If you have integrated with 3rd party payment providers, for example, they will be tested at this stage. Most of the compatibility issues you are likely to face will be uncovered during system test execution.

The final phase is Acceptance Testing. Acceptance Testing is associated with the Business Requirements Analysis phase and involves testing the products in a user's environment by the users. Acceptance tests uncover the compatibility issues with other systems available in the user environments. Acceptance testing also discovers a non-functional issue such as load and performance defects in the user environments.

Where Is the V-Model Suitable?

The V-Model is similar to Waterfall as both models follow a defined path through their stages. To make the V-Model as successful as possible, you will need to make sure your project requirements are well-defined, documented, and thought out so that they don't change over time. You also need to be sure that a product definition is stable. This is much easier to describe than put into practice, project changes over time due to a change in the company's priorities or market conditions are the main reason for problems here. The technology being used must be well understood before you get to the coding phase, there's often no margin for your developers to learn on the job, due to the need to deliver to tight timescales.

Once you leave the Requirements Analysis and Definition phases, you cannot have any ambiguous requirements, because like waterfall there is simply no margin for changing them later without causing a lot of disruption.

Finally, as with Waterfall, the V-Model is ideally suited to shorter project timescales. The longer the project runs, the more risk is introduced of the requirements changing over time.

Advantages and Disadvantages of the V-Model

The V-Model shares very similar advantages and disadvantages of the more traditional Waterfall model, but it is worth covering them again, as it helps set the scene for our discussion about agile software development. The first advantage is that the V-Model is quite easy to understand and apply. It fits well with companies that have different departments all feeding into the development process. The V-Model is also easy to manage, as you only proceed to the next phase of the model once the current phase is complete. This makes it easier for project managers who manage the project. Again, as with Waterfall, the V-Model is not flexible to changes in requirements. This means you'll have to repeat the phases in the models to make sure all your documentation is intact. A shift of needs can be quite disruptive to a project, so you need to ensure the requirements are right from the start.

In reality, what often happens is that if there are any changes to the requirements, to reduce the cost of disruption, the process is just bypassed to get the changes through quicker. If you're going to circumvent a process, there's no point in having the process in the first place?

The V-Model works best on small projects where the risk of changing requirements is less than that of a larger project. The V-Model is easy to understand, and the actual validation phases are suitable for mature test departments. Project managers tend to like the V-Model as it is easier to manage against the plan. The rigidity of the model maps well to a project manager's view of the world and makes their job a bit easier.

The V-Model can introduce a high level of risk and uncertainty for anything but a small project. Just because a set of requirements in design has been signed off, does not mean the conditions cannot change. The V-Model is all about getting the requirements, design, and implementation right the first time, which is a grand ideal, but in the real world this is an infrequent case, and this is a significant risk to a project. I talked about how the V-Model is better for small projects, but it is possible to have a small but very complex project. The more complexity that is involved increases the risk of change being needed further down the line. Complexity in a system is also very hard to implement and test and can often cause delays in the later stages of the V-Model software development lifecycle.

If you're working on a project where change is expected, then a V-Model is not the right model for you. Once you're starting to test your solution, going back to make changes in the code, other than to fix defects, can be very challenging and expensive. The biggest disadvantage of V-Model is that you don't get any working software until late in the process. This means that your end users don't get to see their vision come to life until it is too late to change anything. It can be tough for non-technical people to be clear about what they want an application to do, and it isn't normally until they can visualize the application that they can give excellent feedback.

Agile Software Development

What Is Agile?

Agile software development is a set of software development practices that promote an evolutionary design with teams that can self-organize themselves. Agile software development inspires evolutionary development, adaptive planning methods and early delivery of value from your software to your end customers.

The word agile was first linked to the development of software back in 2001 when the Agile Manifesto was devised by a group of visionary leaders and software developers.

Unlike traditional development practices like the waterfall, agile methodologies such as Scrum and Extreme Programming are focused around self-organizing, cross-discipline teams who practice continuous planning and implementation to deliver value to their customers.

The primary goal of agile software development is to deliver working software that gives value sooner to the end user. Each of these methods emphasizes ongoing association between technology and the business for whom you are developing the software. Agile software methodologies are considered lightweight in that they strive to impose a minimum process and overhead within the development lifecycle.

Agile methods are adaptive which means support changes in requirements and business priorities throughout the whole software construction process. Changes in requirements are to be embraced and welcomed. With an agile software development project, there is also a considerable emphasis on empowering teams with collaborative decision-making. In the previous chapter, I talked about how the Waterfall-based development process follows a set series of stages which results in a "big bang" deployment of software at the end of the process.

One of the main ideas behind Agile software development is that instead of delivering a "big bang" release into production at the end of the project, you release multiple versions of working code to your stakeholders continually. This will allow you to prioritize features that will deliver the most value to the users sooner so that your organization can get an early return on their investment, and that investment comes in the form of money spent and time consumed in development and planning. The number of deliveries into production that you do depends on how long and complicated a project is, but ideally, you would deliver working software at the end of each sprint or iteration.

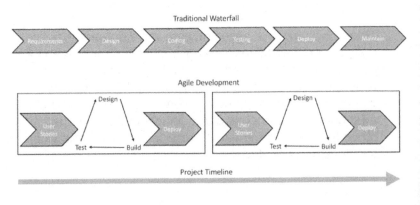

Agile vs Waterfall

Another good way to visualize the premise of Agile is the above diagram. What this diagram shows is that with Agile you deliver incrementally instead of all at once. You should hold this thought in your mind as we progress through the rest of the book.

A Brief History of Agile

There have been lots of attempts to improve software development methodologies over the years, and many of these have looked at working iteratively, these new practices didn't go far enough when trying to deal with changing requirements of customers.

In the 1990's, a group of industry software thought leaders met at a ski resort in Utah to seek and define a better way of developing software. The term "agile software development" emerged from this gathering. The term was first used in this manner and published in the now-famous Agile Manifesto. The agile manifesto was designed to promote the ideas of delivering regular business value to your customers and made it necessary that you should focus on a collaborative, cross-functional team to make this happen.

The Agile Manifesto 4 Core Values

The Agile Manifesto is split into 4 core values.

1. Individuals and interactions over processes and tools
2. Working software over comprehensive documentation
3. Customer collaboration over contract negotiation

4. Responding to change over following a plan

For the first of the core values, we have "Individuals and interactions over processes and tools." People build software systems, and to do this properly, they all need to work together and have good communication between all parties. This isn't just software developers but includes QA, business analysts, project managers, business sponsors, and senior leadership, and anyone else involved in the project at your organization. Processes and tools are necessary but are irrelevant if the people working on the project can't communicate and work together efficiently.

For the second of the core values, we have, "Working software over comprehensive documentation." Let's face it, who reads a 100-page product spec? I certainly don't. Your business users would much prefer to have small pieces of functionality that are delivered quickly so they can then provide feedback. These pieces of functionality may even be enough to deploy to production to gain benefit from them early. Not all documentation is bad though. When my teams work on a project, they use Visio or similar tools to produce diagrams, and this is not an exhaustive list, employment environments, database schemas, software layers, and use-case diagrams. We typically print these out on an A3 printer and put them up on the wall, so they are visible to everyone. Small, useful pieces of documentation like this are invaluable. 100-page product specs are not. Nine times out of ten large items of documentation are invalid and out of date before you even finish writing them. Remember, the primary goal is to develop software that gives the business benefit, not extensive documentation.

For the third of the core values, we have, "Customer collaboration over contract negotiation." All the software that you develop should be written with your customer's involvement. To be successful in software development, you need to work with them daily. This means inviting them to your stand-ups, demoing to them regularly, and inviting them to any design meetings. Only the customer can tell you what they want. They may not be able to give you all the technical details, but that is what your team is there for, to collaborate with them, understand their requirements, and to deliver on them.

For the fourth and final of the core values, we have, "Responding to change over following a plan." Your customer or business sponsor may change their minds about what is being built. This may be because you've given them new ideas from the software you delivered in a previous iteration. It may be because the company's priorities have changed, or new regulatory changes come into force. The key thing here is, you should embrace it. Yes, some code might get thrown away and some time may be lost, but if you're working in short iterations, then this time lost is minimized. Change is a reality of software development, a reality that your software process must reflect. There's nothing wrong with having a project plan. In fact, I'd be worried about any project that didn't have one; however, a project plan must be flexible enough to be changed.

Agile Methodology Overview

Which agile project methodologies are commonly in use today?

First of all, we have Scrum. Scrum is a lightweight project management framework that is based on an interactive working model. Ken Schwaber, Mike Beedle, Jeff Sutherland, and others, contributed to the development of Scrum over many years. Over the last few years, Scrum has earned growing popularity in the software development community because of its simplicity, proven success, and improved productivity, and its ability to work with various other engineering practices promoted by other Agile methodologies, such as Extreme Programming.

Next, we have Extreme Programming or XP as it is also known. Extreme Programming was initially devised by Kent Beck and has emerged as one of the more popular and controversial Agile methods. Extreme Programming is a disciplined approach to delivering high-quality software faster and consistently. It emphasizes lots of customer engagement, rapid feedback loops, continuous testing, continuous planning, and teamwork to deliver working software at a frequent release cadence, typically every 1-3 weeks. Whereas Scrum is a project management framework, XP is much more of an engineering discipline. It is very common for teams to adopt Scrum yet borrow different engineering practices from XP.

The original XP recipe is based on four simple values:

1. Simplicity
2. Communication
3. Feedback
4. Courage

There's also 12 supporting practices. These are:

1. Planning game
2. Small releases
3. Customer acceptance tests
4. Simple design
5. Pair programming

6. Test-driven development
7. Refactoring
8. Continuous integration
9. Collective code ownership
10. Coding standards
11. Metaphors
12. Sustainable pace

Next, we have the Crystal methodology. The Crystal Method is a lightweight, adaptable approach to software development. Crystal is comprised of a family of methods like Crystal Clear, Crystal Yellow, and Crystal Orange, whose unique characteristics are driven by factors, like team size, system criticality, and project priorities. The Crystal family looks at the fact that each software project may require a different set of policies, processes, and practices to meet the project's requirements.

Next, we have the Dynamic Systems Development Method, or DSDM as it is most commonly known. DSDM dates back to 1994 and evolved to provide an industry standard project framework for what was commonly called rapid application development or RAD for short.

While RAD was famous in the early 1990's, the RAD approach was quite unstructured and as a result of this DSDM was formulated to add structure to the idea of rapid application development. Since 1994, DSDM has evolved to provide a comprehensive foundation for managing, planning, executing, and scaling agile and iterative software development projects. DSDM is based on nine key principles that revolve around business need and value, active user involvement, empowered teams, frequent delivery, integration testing, and business stakeholder collaboration.

Then we have Feature-Driven Design or FDD for short. Jeff De Luca originally developed the feature-driven design. FDD is a model-driven, short-iteration process. It begins with establishing an overall model shape; then it continues with a series of 2-week, design-by-feature, built-by-feature iterations. The features are small and useful in the eyes of the client. FDD designs the rest of the development process around feature delivery using the following eight practices:

1. Domain object modeling
2. Developing by feature
3. Components and class ownership
4. Feature teams
5. Inspections
6. Configuration management
7. Regular builds
8. Visibility of progress
9. Results

Next, we have Lean software development. Lean software development is an iterative method initially developed by Mary and Tom Poppendieck. Lean software development owes its heritage to the Lean enterprise movement of companies like Toyota. Lean software development focuses heavily on the team to deliver value to the customer and on the efficiency of the value stream and the mechanisms that provide that value.

The main principles of Lean include:

- Eliminating waste
- Amplifying learning
- Deciding as late as possible
- Delivering as fast as possible
- Empowering the team
- Building in integrity
- Seeing the whole

Lean eliminates waste by focusing on only parts of a system that deliver real value to businesses. Lean Software Development puts emphasis on the speed and efficiency of development and relies on rapid feedback between programmers and customers.

Roles within an Agile Team

Agile teams, while part of a department or company, are primarily focused on their software development goals. Each team should also be focused on their team's overall vision. This means a team should be very reactive in doing whatever is required to get the job done. This means that team members may have to do work that is outside their usual skill set. This should be embraced and encouraged. A cross-functional and adaptive team is much more likely to succeed.

Most teams will, of course, have some standard areas of expertise and specialisms and you may also have people with the particular domain or product knowledge, but there should be flexibility in team players expected roles and responsibilities. It should also be common for team members to have access to the business as a whole and this shouldn't just be limited to a select few. You should have people who are tasked with making sure the team follows the development process and someone who co-ordinates requirements gathering with the business, this would typically be referred to like the product owner if you are working within the Scrum framework.

Teams will normally have some form of a leadership role within the team. In Scrum, this person is the Scrum master. On Agile teams, this person aims to enable and ensure the success of the team. This type of leader is frequently referred to as a servant leader. This role is entirely different to the direct transactional leader on a Waterfall project.

One goal of an agile team should be to improve as a team every day. The larger the organization, the more complicated group structures can get. Cross-project teams, shared services, operations, configuration management, and database administration can all come into play, but the goal remains the same, define a software project and cross-functional team capable of delivering on that plan and empower the team to do so.

Common Agile Misconceptions

Agile Misconceptions

When a team is new to agile, it can be hard for them to adjust to a new way of working, especially if they're used to working under a Waterfall-based methodology. When a team is faced with changing how they work, it is common for excuses to be made by team members as they resist the change. Not all teams are like this, but in my experience, it is quite common to hear many different misconceptions, in this chapter we'll discuss many of these mistakes and why they come about.

Agile is ad-hoc, with no process control: To be agile, you need to adhere to the Agile Manifesto, but following the manifesto doesn't mean you are using a defined process. The manifesto describes a set of ideas. There are various processes and project management templates that you can apply to your projects to help them become agile. Extreme Programming and Scrum are the two most popular, but Lean and Kanban are also becoming very popular.

When you try to implement the manifesto items, you generally need to apply lots of common sense and pragmatism to help you get to your goal, but if you want to warp a more formal process around the "how" of agile, as opposed to the "why", then you would need to apply something like Scrum or Extreme Programming, which gives you more formal processes like stories, iterations, stand-ups, demos, retrospectives, test-driven development, and pair programming.

Agile is wasteful without upfront planning: This assumes that your customer knows the details of all their requirements in advance. If this is true, then by all means, undertake comprehensive upfront planning. However, in reality, this is rare and usually, leads to greater waste of having taken design and development work that was ultimately unnecessary.

Agile development is not predictable: When working with an established agile team, you can bring a level of predictability to your development life-cycle and business as you will be regularly delivering working software to your customers. The frequency of these releases will be set with your stakeholders, but in the ideal situation, you should have releasable code at the end of each sprint.

Agile is faster and cheaper: Running an Agile team doesn't mean you will finish a project quicker or for less money. It isn't a direct money saver in that respect. What being agile is about is delivering value to the business sooner. You head toward working versions of the software quicker. At the end of each development iteration, you're supposed to have working software to demo to the business. You may not have all their requirements in place, but what is there will work. This means re-thinking about how you plan your workload in each iteration. Instead of delivering horizontal slices, for example, the data access layers this iteration and user interface in the next iteration, you think in vertical segments.

This means you deliver defined pieces of functionality in an iteration that may encompass work on the user interface and data access layer. It's a mind shift change that I've seen teams struggle with if they are used to working horizontally, but when they finally get it, the efficiency of a team is increased remarkably. Being agile is also about being able to respond to change. Requirements can vary, and business can change partway through delivery. I've worked with teams who treat this is a real negative thing. If you want to be agile, you need to expect and embrace that things will change. The tools and processes of Scrum, for example, are designed to help you react to these changes in a more efficient manner.

Agile teams don't write documents or do planning: Practising agile on your team is not an excuse to avoid planning or documentation writing. Agile is an act of doing what is needed at the time of requiring it, and encourages continuous planning and documentation, but only when it is necessary for specific customer requirements. This allows teams along with their customers to decide if the plan or document adds value to the product. Depending on what type of company you work for, formal documentation may not be something that you can avoid. For example, if you work in a very densely regulated environment, then there's lots of upfront documentation that may be needed for evidence and submission to a regulatory body. If this is the case, then the delivery team will need to take this documentation into account.

I prefer to work with large diagrams instead of large documents of text. If you can, get these diagrams printed out onto A3 paper, and then put them up all over the walls, so you have something to refer to in your standups. With the planning side of this, you still need to do it. At the beginning of each iteration or sprint, you should have a planning session where you allocate user stories for iteration. The number of stories you allocate will be based on the estimates given and the velocity of the previous iteration.

Agile means no commitments: It can be a common belief that people on agile teams do not want to make promises and that you have a team of developers churning away until someone shouts "We're Done!" A successful agile team should be very transparent about what they intend to deliver to their users. When using methodologies like Scrum and Extreme Programming you have a concept of a backlog which contains all your high-level user stories and tasks for a given sprint or iteration. As you define the workload for a sprint, this should be seen as a guide to what the team intends to deliver. Once a sprint or iteration is setup, it will not change, but it may be required that you have to change your plan part way through a sprint. This could result in a partial re-plan in that sprint/iteration or wait until the next sprint. XP doesn't like changing a sprint once it is in flight, and this is more acceptable under Scrum, but no law says you cannot alter the commitment if required. What is important is that a level of trust is built up between the team and the business stakeholders.

An agile project will never end: This might be true in some situations. You should continue to work on a project while the customer continues to get business value. Most products in any industry have a point of diminishing returns. This is the ideal time for an agile project to end. This decision should come from the business though, for it is them that you are delivering value to. Agile works for projects, teams, and organizations of any size, not just small projects. This doesn't mean it'll necessarily work for all teams, but size is rarely a factor. Large and complex projects and organizations are often excellent candidates for an agile transformation, where it is difficult or impossible to know all of your customer's requirements in advance.

Agile is the solution to all your problems: Agile is a change in approach and culture that comes with its own set of benefits and issues. If you're working in a well-established team that has not been following any agile processes, then changing them over will not be an instant transformation. You need to do it slowly, make sure everyone has a say in decision-making. If you don't, you may get resistance from team members who fear change, which is a perfectly normal human characteristic. Convincing your team isn't the biggest hurdle though, your biggest challenge is making sure that your leadership team understands and wants to adopt Agile as a way of working. Once you have achieved this and had leadership buy-in, then the rest of the adoption just takes time and patience as everyone adjusts.

There's only one way to do agile: The original Agile Manifesto consists of four core values and 12 principles. It doesn't document any actual implementation details. There are many interpretations of Agile that form different methodologies, like Scrum, Extreme Programming, Kanban, and Feature-Driven Development, to name a few. Each style has its benefits and weaknesses, and you must evaluate your situations to decide which methodology is the best fit for your team. Extreme Programming and Scrum are the two most popular methods in use today, but also Lean, and Kanban are becoming very popular. As long as you stick to the Agile Manifesto's values and principles and deliver high-value software regularly to your customers, you should be considered agile.

Agile development doesn't require upfront design: It is a common misconception that agile teams just make it up as they go along. This isn't true, what is more, realistic is that agile teams should make sure design happens at the last responsible point in time. For coding activities, it is more acceptable that the code is designed as the developer works on it and refactors to a better design as they go along, this is what evolutionary design is all about. More system-wide and architectural design can be scheduled in 1 or more sprints/iterations ahead of time. By only designing as you need to, you can react to changes in requirements more efficiently. When you try to design the entire system up front, any design decisions that you make are likely to be redundant by the time you come to implement them.

Advantages and Disadvantages

Advantages of Agile

As you've seen in the past chapters, agile software development is an entirely different approach to software development compared to the more traditional Waterfall development model. Let's take a look at some of the advantages to using Agile as an approach.

Customer satisfaction by rapid, continuous delivery of useful software: Your clients and users will be satisfied because you are continually delivering value to them with usable software. This is a stark contrast compared to that of the traditional Waterfall product delivery process. Now if your customers are used to Waterfall, they may find it strange adjusting to having working software sooner. The big downside of Waterfall is that you deliver large pieces of functionality towards the end of the project life-cycle. This means all throughout the development stages of Waterfall your project is incurring the cost with no return on investment. By delivering working pieces of functionality sooner and more regularly, you're giving your users an opportunity to get a return on their investment sooner. Sure, they may not have all the functionality they need up front, but they can start to make use of the solution to make their lives easier and start realizing the benefits sooner. People and interactions are emphasized rather than process and tools.

Agile is focused very heavily on people and the interactions between people rather than the processes and tools: This is a core value of the Agile Manifesto. The reason this is important is that it is the input from your team and customers that will ultimately make your project a success, as opposed to what tools you use. Continual collaboration throughout the entire development cycle of your project enables everyone involved to build up a good working relationship that will be based on trust. This trust-based working relationship is crucial when building software incrementally.

Continuous attention to high-quality code: When working with Agile, you're working short iterations and only build what is necessary to satisfy the requirements for that iteration and nothing else. This forces you to keep your design simple, which is essential as simplicity helps you develop testable, and therefore, more reliable systems. Developers understand and choose many solutions to solve a business's problem, and these are choices that reflect a craft that balances design, use, and support. Developers provide the technical assistance to the team that enables them always to keep code quality high. Developers like to use the latest techniques for keeping their implementations straightforward and clean without having to rework any of their solutions.

Some of these techniques include refactoring. Refactoring is the process of improving the design of existing code without changing its behavior. To make changes to the structure of the code, refactoring uses a quick succession of small, well-defined steps that can be verified as safe or functionally equivalent. Refactoring is most often done in conjunction with test-driven development where unit tests and simple design make it easier to refactor safely.

Simple design: Keeping your design simple, and not repeating code, helps you keep a level of maintainability for your system. If you design your code to be modular, then you can reduce coupling between objects, which leads to an overall, more robust system.

Test-driven development: Test-driven development is a way of improving the design of your code by writing unit tests, which expresses what you intend the code to do, making that test pass, and continually refactoring to keep the design as simple as possible. TDD can be applied at multiple levels, for example, unit tests and integration tests. Test-driven development follows a rigorous cycle. You start by writing a failing test. Then you implement the most straightforward solution that will make that test to pass. Then you search for duplication in the code and remove it. This is often called Red-Green-Refactor and has become almost a mantra for many test-driven design practitioners. Understanding and even internalizing this cycle is key to being able to use test-driven design to solve your problems.

Embracing changes in requirements: Your clients or business partners may want to change their mind about the software that is being built. This might be because you have inspired them with new ideas from the software you delivered in a previous iteration. It could be because the company's priorities have changed. The key thing here is that you should embrace the change. Yes, some code may get thrown away and some time is lost, but if you're working in short iterations, then this lost time is minimized.

Change can be terrifying at first for clients and partners alike, but when both sides are prepared to leap, it can be mutually rewarding. In some ways, Agile is a simple idea, but the reality is that it can mean different things to different people, especially depending on their role in the software development process. One of the key things, though, is to be open to change, not just to move in traditional ways of organizing projects but to adapt your use of Agile itself.

Early return on investments: Another advantage to releasing features early is you get a return on your investment sooner. Running a software development team is expensive. You have permanent developers and testers, as well as consultants with expensive day rates. There's also business analysts, project managers, as well as other hardware and software costs. These are all costs to the business. By releasing early and generating revenue from your product, you can start to offset some of the initial investment and development costs. On the flip side of that, if you have a more Waterfall-based approach where you end up with a "big bang" deployment after a year or so, you will have already spent significant amounts of money to fund the development with nothing to show until at the end.

Feedback from your customers: If you release early, this means you can start to solicit feedback from your clients a lot sooner. These customers could be public-facing customers or business sponsors. I've worked on many projects where the business customer specifies requirements, which you then build, only for the customer to want changes once they have something they can use. This always seems to happen. It's tough for someone to specify a system without having something to play with.

You can use prototyping software to help, but there is nothing like giving them actual functionality early on to start using. One of the principles of Agile is to embrace change in the requirements. This should be expected, so giving your customer something they can feedback on sooner will allow them an opportunity to make changes sooner without causing much disruption.

Feedback from real customers: Once you start getting feedback from real customers, you can start incorporating changes and new ideas from the feedback into the product. It is much more cost effective to make changes early on in a product's development cycle than it is to wait until the end once a large release has been achieved. It's not just customer feedback that helps you build the right product, by testing your product early in the marketplace, you can gauge customer uptake and see how popular the product will be, and continually deliver better quality.

Everything we have discussed so far has business benefits or culminates in the fact that you should be providing a better-quality product with every release. By releasing earlier and soliciting feedback, you can learn from the product performance earlier, and use this information to create something of higher quality. Product and system development are all about continuous learning and improvement, which is much easier to do when you're delivering a project by being agile. It doesn't matter whether you're using Extreme Programming, Scrum, DSDM, Crystal, or any of the other project management frameworks. If you stick to the core values in the Agile Manifesto and routinely deliver high-value functionality early to your customers, monitor their usage and listen to their feedback, you can apply this learning to the ongoing development and increase quality as you go along.

Disadvantages of Agile

Now that we have taken a look at some of the advantages let's now take a look at some disadvantages.

Hard to assess the effort required at the beginning of the software development life cycle: One complaint I have often heard from business leaders and project managers alike, is that compared to Waterfall, it is hard to quantify the total effort and cost to deliver a project. On the one hand, I can see why they would think this, especially when they come from a regimented Waterfall process world. Indeed, it is harder to quantify how long the total project will take entirely, but the mitigation for this is that a product will be delivered incrementally by giving the users the most valuable requirements first, meaning you can plan for the coming sprint and maybe a few sprints ahead to provide a specified amount of functionality.

It can be very demanding on a users' time: Active user participation and collaboration with the users of your system are required throughout the development cycle with Agile. This can be very rewarding and ensures you deliver the right product to your users. It's an essential principle with Agile to make sure that a user's expectations are well-managed, and the definition of failure is not meeting your user's expectations. However, this level of participation can be very demanding on the user and require a big commitment for the duration of the project. I have been in this situation many times where the business users love the idea of what Agile can bring to them, but they don't like the extra amount of time they have to spend on the project as they have to still fit this in with their current workloads.

Costs can increase as testers are required all the time instead of at the end of a project: Testing is an essential part of an agile project during sprints or iterations. This helps to ensure quality throughout the project without the need for a lengthy and unpredictable test phase at the end of a project. However, this does mean that testers are needed throughout the entire product development lifecycle, and this can dramatically increase the cost of resources on your team. This extra upfront cost does save you money in the long run though as you are continually having people test your code. Having a combination of manual testing and automation testing is the best way to drive up the quality of your product. The cost of a long and unpredictable test stage at the end of a waterfall project can, in my experience, cause enormous unexpected losses when the project overruns, and they frequently do overrun.

What Are Your Department's Biggest Challenges?

Let's now take a look at whether Agile is right for your team, and if you are prepared for moving to a more agile way of working. If you are working at a new company or on a brand-new team, starting out with Agile can be very easy, but if you're working in a larger, well-established organization that has been using more of a Waterfall-based approach, the switch to Agile can be challenging to do.

Let's start off by looking at possible challenges faced by your department.

Is your department under pressure to achieve hard deadlines? Are there too few people to get the work done, or insufficient budget allocations? Are staff not as productive as they could or should be? Are the business processes, equipment or communication channels that they use slowing them down? Is there too much corporate knowledge in the heads of a handful of employees, or are low-quality outputs creating the need for constant fire-fighting and damage control? Every IT team can benefit from using agile approaches, but the teams that have the most significant issues also have the most to gain from agile approaches that specifically target these issues. This is why agile methods are ideally suited to teams where there are ongoing problems with the quality of delivered solutions, providing software solutions within agreed timelines and budgets, delivered solutions not adequately supporting business requirements, or high staff turnover rates or low staff productivity levels.

The amount of benefit your team will get from implementing Agile is also linked to some risks.

- The likely hood for requirements changing while the product is being developed, and this includes changes in user needs, staff departures, business priority shifts, and funding.

- External changes where there are variations in the market demand, announcements from competitors, and the availability of new technologies

- The sustainability of your current overheads, including development costs, implementation costs, maintenance, and support.

If your products are based on predictable and replicable business processes with a minimum likelihood of changing requirements, then your team will not achieve the same level of benefit from Agile as one that is more susceptible to solution requirements that are likely to evolve. The same goes for teams where the current software solutions are delivered on time, align well with the business requirements, and require minimal ongoing support to address quality and usability issues. In each of these situations, Agile methodologies can provide some degree of benefit to the team, but not the dramatic benefit that the teams with more dynamic and less sustainable software solutions can achieve. Ultimately, the more your team is faced with changing requirements, and unsustainable IT overheads, the better positioned you are to receive returns on your Agile investments.

Are You Prepared for Agile?

For some organizations, notably larger and older ones, the answer to the question, are your people prepared for change, is likely to be no.

The idea of implementing methodologies that encourage the evolution of business requirements instead of relying on upfront documentation, empowering the project team to self-organize instead of controlling their daily activities, and replacing reams of documentation with face-to-face communication may seem a bit daunting for some staff. This is particularly the case for those that have grown comfortable with their normal day to day routines and just live with the problems in their code and the solution they are developing. A great debilitation when trying agile is people saying, "This is the way we have always done it." These types of individuals are usually very resistant to change.

If your staff is hesitant at first, you may find that giving agile a try on a donor project in your team will help get them familiar with and motivated by agile. If after trying one or two agile projects your staff is still uncomfortable working directly with the business areas, supporting changing requirements as the project progresses, and self-managing their work, it may be that agile approaches are just not suited to your organization's working culture.

If on the other hand, your team reacts well to the trial projects then this paves the way for you more fully adopting these methodologies. Going agile does require a change in attitude for managers and leadership too. Traditionally it might have been more common to have direct control over what your team members are working on, but with agile you need to take a different approach.

Management style needs to be more like servant leadership where managers are there to remove any barriers from the teams' progress and encourage the team to think for themselves and organize their workload. After all, developers are paid very well, so you need to have a more realistic level of trust that they will do the right thing.

Another interesting thing about the dynamic of self-organizing teams is that as they progress, they improve ongoing motivation for employees. Project team members know that their continued ability to self-manage their work depends on their regular delivery of higher-value business outcomes. Additionally, because they are the ones who identify what work can and cannot be achieved in each iteration, they are motivated by their responsibility to reach these outcomes. This combination of factors is heightened by the satisfaction and pride that staff members feel when they produce tangible outputs that truly meet the needs of the organization.

Extreme Programming (XP)

Now that we have looked at some theory of agile software development, it's time now to take a look at some agile methodologies.

In this chapter, we'll look at Extreme Programming or XP for short. As we look at Extreme Programming, we'll first look at its history; then we'll look at an overview of the methodology, following that we'll look at the typical Extreme Programming activities, values, principles, and practices. Finally, we'll finish up by looking at the different rules of Extreme Programming, which are split down into five categories, planning, managing, designing, coding, and testing.

History of Extreme Programming

Extreme Programming is a methodology in Software Development which promotes improving software quality and being able to respond to changing customer requirements. As an agile methodology, it supports more frequent releases to your end users and shorter development cycles. Other elements of Extreme Programming include programming in pairs or doing extensive code reviews, unit testing all of the code and avoiding programming of features until they are needed.

The name Extreme Programming comes from the idea that software engineering practices are taken to extreme levels within your team. For example, code reviews are a good practice, and under intense programming, they are taken to an absolute level by promoting continuous code reviewing by pair programming.

Kent Beck was the creator of Extreme Programming during his employment at the then-struggling Chrysler Comprehensive Compensation System payroll project or C3 as it was known in 1996. The project was designed to aggregate many different payroll systems into a single application.

Initially, Chrysler attempted to implement a solution, but it failed because of the complexity surrounding the rules and integration. From this point of crisis, Kent Beck and his team took over, effectively starting the project from scratch. The classic Waterfall development approach had been tried and failed, so something drastic was required. In Kent Beck's own words regarding Extreme Programming, he just made the whole thing up in two weeks with a marker in his hand and a whiteboard. Fundamentally, the C3 team focused on the business value the customer wanted and discarded anything that did not work towards that goal. Developers created extreme Programming for developers.

The XP team at Chrysler were able to deliver their first working system within one year. In 1997, the first 10,000 employees were paid from the new C3 system. Development continued over the next year with new functionality being added through smaller releases. Eventually, the project was cancelled because the prime contractor changed, and the focus of Chrysler shifted away from C3. When the dust settled, the 8-member development team had built a system with 2,000 classes and 30,000 methods. XP had been refined and tested and was now ready for the wider development community.

Overview of Extreme Programming

Extreme Programming can be described as a software development discipline that organizes people to produce high-quality software more productively. Extreme Programming attempts to reduce the cost of changing requirements by having multiple short development cycles rather than one long cycle as is seen in Waterfall.

With Extreme Programming, changes are a natural, inescapable, and desirable aspect of software development projects. You should plan and expect changes in requirements, instead of thinking you will get a complete and stable set of requirements upfront that will not change. Extreme Programming also introduces four activities such as coding, testing, listening, and designing. There are also five values, such as communication, simplicity, feedback, courage, and respect, four principles, such as feedback, assuming simplicity, and embracing change.

There are also 12 practices that are split into four groups. These groups are fine-scale feedback, continuous process, shared understanding, and programmer welfare. And finally, there are 29 rules divided into the following five groups. These groups are planning, managing, designing, coding, and testing. We will cover all these activities, practices and rules in the remainder of the chapter.

Activities

Extreme Programming describes four primary activities that are performed within the software development process.

These activities are

- Coding
- Testing
- Listening
- Designing

Coding

Coding is an essential product of the Extreme Programming process. Without code, there is no working product. To a programmer, a well written and structured system serves as good documentation to his or her fellow programmers. This coding can involve many different languages such as C#, Java, Python, C, C++, F#, JavaScript, and much more.

Testing

With Extreme Programming, the developer will practice what is called test-driven development. This is where you write a failing test first and implement just enough code to pass the test, and then refactor the code to a better structure, while tests still pass. The programmer will strive to cover as much of their code in unit tests as they can to give them a good level of overall code coverage. This code coverage will help build up the trust that the system operates as expected.

You cannot be sure of having a working system or product unless you have tested it. With Extreme Programming, you ideally want to automate as much of your testing as possible so that you can repeat the testing frequently. This can be done by writing unit tests. Unit tests will test a small block of code in isolation of any external dependencies like databases or the file system.

Listening

The next activity to discuss is that of listening. Programmers must listen to what the customers need the system to do and what business logic is required. The requirements from the customer are documented as a series of user stories.

These user stories help to drive out a series of acceptance tests, which help determine when a user story is completed and working as expected. Once user stories and acceptance tests are written, the developers can then start their planning and estimating.

Designing

The final activity is designing. To create a working system or product, requirement gathering, coding, and testing should be all you need, but in reality, software systems are very complicated, so you'll often need to perform a level of overall system design that you may not have expected. This doesn't mean that you'd to create a several-hundred-page design document, as that could be quite wasteful, but there is definite value in producing an overall system design where you look at the whole structure of the system and its dependencies.

Ideally, you want to create a system where all of the components are as decoupled from each other as they can be so that a change in one part doesn't require sweeping changes across the rest of the system.

Values

There are five core values that Extreme Programming is based on. Although Extreme Programming defines many rules, which we'll look at in a bit, Extreme Programming is more wired to work in harmony with your personal and corporate values. The five values are:

- Communication
- Simplicity
- Feedback
- Respect
- Courage

Communication

For any project to succeed you need to have good communication between the development team and all the stakeholders. By having good communication on the team, it makes it a lot easier for the team to respond to changes in requirements from the end users.

The customer sees the team's progress every day and can adjust the work schedule as needed, as the client collaborates with the developers to produce tests to verify that a feature is present and works as expected.

When you have a question about a feature, you should ask the customer directly. A 5-minute face-to-face conversation, peppered with body language, gestures, and whiteboard drawings, communicates more than an email exchange or conference call can, so removing the communication barriers between customers and developers increases your flexibility.

Clear communication about goals, status, and priorities not only allows you to succeed but makes everything else in the project run smoothly too.

Simplicity

Simplicity means building only the parts of the system that need to be built. It means solving today's problems today and tomorrow's problems tomorrow. Predicting the future is very hard, so building in excessive complexity early on is very costly. Once you're armed with communication and feedback, it's much easier to know what you need. If you practice simplicity, it should be as easy to add a feature when it becomes necessary.

Feedback

Feedback means asking questions and learning from the answers. The only way to know what a customer wants is to ask them. The only way to know if the code does what it should do is to test it. The sooner you can get feedback, the more time you have to react to it. XP provides rapid, frequent feedback. Every XP practice is part of building a feedback loop. The best way to reduce the cost of change is to listen to and learn from all of those sources as often as possible. This is why XP concentrates on frequent planning, design, testing, and communicating. Rapid feedback reduces the investment of time and resources in ideas with little payoff.

Failures are found as soon as possible, within days or weeks rather than months or years, and this feedback helps you to refine your schedule and your plans even further than your original estimates may have ever allowed you to. It will enable you to steer your project back on track as soon as someone notices a problem and identifies when a feature is finished, and very importantly where it will cost more or less than previously believed. It builds confidence that the system does just what the customer wants.

Courage

Making hard decisions can be tough and it takes a lot of courage. If a feature isn't working, fix it. If some code is not up to standard, improve it. If you're not going to deliver everything you promised on schedule, be up front and tell the customer as soon as possible. Courage is a difficult virtue of applying. No one wants to be wrong or to break a promise. The only way to recover from a mistake, though, is to admit it and fix it.

Delivering software is challenging, but meeting that challenge instead of avoiding it, leads to better software.

Respect

Respect within your team underlies the other values previously mentioned. Intrinsic rewards like motivation, enjoyment, and job satisfaction beat extrinsic rewards like employee-of-the-month awards or physical rewards every time. Everyone should contribute value to the team, even if it's simply enthusiasm. Developers should always respect the expertise of the customers and vice-versa, and managers should always respect the developer's right to accept responsibility and receive authority over their work.

Principles

Frequent and prompt feedback is very useful with Extreme Programming as it reduces the cycle time from feedback to action being taken to resolve any feedback. Rapid action on feedback is critical to a team learning through frequent contact with their customers. This also means the customer has a clear insight into the system that is being developed and can give feedback and steer development as needed.

Unit tests contribute significantly to the rapid feedback principle. When writing code, running the unit tests provides direct feedback as to how the system reacts to any changes made to it. If a developer's code changes mean there is a failure in some other part of the system, the automated unit test suites will show the failure immediately, alerting the developer of the incompatibility of his change within other regions of the system, and the necessity of removing or modifying his change.

With software development methodologies like Waterfall, the absence of automated unit tests means that such a code change, thought to be harmless by the developer, would have been left in place, appearing only during integration testing, or even worse showing up once the product has been put into production. Identifying which code changes created the problem, can be a difficult task, and not one you want to perform very often.

Extreme Programming rejects these ideas. Extreme Programming applies small incremental changes to the codebase over time. For example, a system might have small releases every three weeks. When many little steps are made, projects customers and sponsors will have more control over the overall development process and the product being created. As we explored in the agile manifesto, the principle of embracing change is about embracing changes and not working against them.

For instance, if at one of the iteration planning meetings it appears the customer's requirements have changed dramatically, programmers can embrace this and plan new requirements for the next iteration. Under waterfall development, changes in requirements are seen as a hazardous and costly thing to happen. Even small changes can have a very large impact on a program of work. If any of the main fundamental requirements change under Waterfall, it could put the entire project at risk of being cancelled. This risk is drastically minimized under an agile development framework like Extreme Programming.

Practices

In Extreme Programming, 12 practices are followed. These are split into four main groups that aim to define software development best practices. These are:

1. Fine-scale feedback
2. Continuous process
3. Shared understanding
4. Programmer welfare

Fine-scaled Feedback

First up are the practices for fine-scale feedback. First of all, there's pair programming. Pair programming means that all code is produced by two people programming on one task at one workstation. One programmer is writing the code at the keyboard, while the other developer is about the problem being solved and looking at the big picture. This programmer is also reviewing the code that the other developer is writing.

Programmers trade roles after short periods of time. The pairs are not fixed. Developers switch partners frequently so that everyone has good coverage over the whole codebase. This way, pair programming can also enhance team-wide communication.

The planning game is the primary planning process for Extreme Programming. The game is a meeting that occurs once per iteration, typically once a week or every two weeks. The planning game is broken into two parts. First, there is release planning. This is focused on determining what requirements are included in which near-term releases, and when they should be delivered. The customers and the developers are both parts of this meeting.

Release planning consists of three phases. The first is the exploration phase where the customer will provide a list of requirements for the product. These will be documented on what are called story cards. Then there's the commitment phase. Within this phase, the customer and developers will commit to what functionality will be delivered and in what time frame.

Then there's the steering phase. In this period, the plan can be adjusted, new requirements can be added, and conditions can be changed or removed. After release planning, we have iteration planning where the tasks for the developers are defined. In this process, the customer is not involved. The primary purpose of the planning game is to help guide the product into delivery. Instead of predicting the exact dates when deliverables will be needed and produced, which is difficult to do, the aim is to steer the project to completion.

Then we have test-driven development. Unit tests are code-based tests that exercise the functionality of the system being developed. Within Extreme Programming, unit tests are defined before the code is written. This helps the programmer think through the possible failure scenarios for the system that needs to be implemented.

First, developers write a minimal test that should break because the functionality hasn't been fully implemented yet. Then the developers verify that the code does indeed fail the test. Then they will write the minimum amount of code to make the test pass. Then the unit tests are run to make sure that they pass. You should then modify or restructure the code to a better design while the tests still pass.

Within XP, the customer is the one who uses the system being developed. Extreme Programming says that the customer should be on hand at all times and available for questions. For instance, a team developing a healthcare dispensing system should include a pharmacy business partner to answer questions and assist with the design.

Continuous Process

Now let's take a look at the practices for a continuous process. First, we have continuous integration. The development team always needs to be working on the latest version of the software by using a source code repository like TFS or Git.

The source code repository should ideally run an automated build against the code as it is checked in and then run the automated unit tests. This will test the integrity of the code being submitted to the repository. Continuous integration of the source code in the repository will avoid delays later on in the product life-cycle caused by integration problems.

Next, we have refactoring or design improvements. XP advocates programming only what is needed today and implementing it as simply as possible. Another symptom is that changes in one part of the code affect lots of other parts, Extreme Programming states that when this happens, the codebase is informing you to refactor your code by changing the design which makes it simpler and more generic.

The delivery of the software is done by frequent releases of functionality creating value for the end user. Small releases help the customer to gain confidence in the progress of the project over time. Once you're building quality software, the whole team as a unit can feel good about the accomplishments they've achieved.

Shared Understanding

Coding standards are an agreed upon set of rules that the entire development team agrees to adhere to throughout the project. The standards specify a consistent style and format for source code within a chosen programming language, as well as various programming constructs and patterns that should be avoided to reduce the probability of defects.

The coding standards may be a set of conventions specified by the language vendor or custom-defined by the development team. These days, it's common to use a coding productivity tool such as ReSharper, CodeRush, or JustCode to help enforce these standards. These tools will be set up with a pre-defined set of rules, and as the developer is writing code, these tools will highlight violations of the coding standards, and in most cases, offer suggestions for fixes. They are excellent for ensuring consistency within a code base.

Next, we have collective code ownership, which means that everyone on the team is responsible for all of the code. This, in turn, means that everybody is allowed to change any part of the code. Pair programming contributes to this practice by working different pairs. All the programmers get to see all of the parts of the code.

A significant advantage of collective code ownership is that it speeds up the development process because when any errors are detected, then any developer can go in and fix them. By giving every programmer the right to modify the code, there is a higher risk of defects being introduced by developers who think they know what they're doing but do not foresee certain dependencies. Sufficiently well-defined unit tests help to address this problem. If unforeseen dependencies create errors, then when the unit tests are run they will show up as failures.

Next up we have, simple design. A keep it simple mentality should be approached when designing a system. Whenever a new piece of code is developed, the programmers should ask themselves, is there a simpler way to create the same functionality. If the answer is yes, then the more straightforward approach should be adopted.

Finally, with a shared understanding, we have the system metaphor. The system metaphor is a story that everyone, customers, programmers, and managers, can tell about how the system works. It's a naming concept for classes and methods that should make it easier for a team member to guess the functionality of a particular class or method from its name only. For example, a pharmacy healthcare system may create a dispensable drugs class for a dispensing system, and if the drug goes out of stock, then the system will return a warning when a check stock availability method is called on the dispensing drug's class. For each class or operation, the functionality is obvious to the entire team.

Programmer Welfare

For the final principle, we'll take a look at programmer welfare and start with sustainable pace. By this, we mean that a developer should not work more than 40 hours in a week, and if they do have to do overtime one week, they shouldn't be expected to do overtime the following week. Extreme Programming projects utilize short iterations that make use of continuous integration, which means more value can be delivered to the business sooner than with more traditional waterfall development. Due to this fact XP projects produce more in at a steadier pace instead of having to have a mad rush at the end. A key enabler to achieve sustainable pace is to frequently merge code and always have an executable version of the product that is well tested with unit tests.

Well-tested, continuously integrated, frequently-deployed code and environments also minimize the frequency of unexpected production problems and outages and the associated after-hours, nights, and weekend work that is required.

Rules

The first version of the rules for Extreme Programming were published in 1999 by Don Wells. 29 rules are given in the categories of:

- Planning
- Managing
- Designing
- Coding
- Testing

Planning

The first category is planning. The first rule in this category is that user stories are written. User stories are used to document the use cases for the system being built. They are also used to create time estimates for the release planning meeting. User stories are used instead of large requirements documents, and they are written by the customers as requirements and functionality that the system needs to perform.

They are in the format of about three sentences of text written by the client in the customer's language. The user stories are not meant to be technical. User stories also help drive the creation of the acceptance tests. One or more automated acceptance tests should be created to verify the user story has been correctly implemented.

A planning meeting is used to create a release plan for the product. This plan is then used to break the release down into multiple iterations. It is essential in this meeting for technical people to make technical decisions, and business people to make business decisions. The idea of this release planning session is for the development team to estimate how long each user story will take to implement in ideal programming weeks. An ideal week is how long you imagine it would take to develop that story if you had absolutely nothing else to do and no distractions. The customer then prioritizes each story by their relative importance and value added to the system.

The development team should be aiming to release iterative and working version of the system to their customers often. Some development teams will deploy software into production every day. But more commonly, you'll want to deploy software into production every one or two weeks.

At the end of every iteration, the development team should have tested, working, and production-ready software to demonstrate to customers. The customers will then decide whether to put that release into production. The iterative development adds agility to the development process. Divide your development schedule into a series of iterations of 1-3 weeks in length. You should keep the iteration length consistent, as this sets the pace for your product like a beating drum.

You shouldn't schedule programming tasks in advance. Instead, you use the iteration planning meetings at the start of each iteration to decide the priority for what will be done. Just-in-time planning is a more natural way to stay on top of changing user requirements.

Any failed acceptance tests from the previous iteration are also selected to be fixed in the next iteration. The customer chooses stories that have estimates that total out to the project velocity of the last iteration. The velocity is the average amount of work that can be completed in each iteration. The user stories and failed tests are broken down into the programming tasks that will support them. Programming tasks are written for each user story. While user stories are in the customer's language, tasks are in the developer's language.

Managing

Good communication is crucial for an Extreme Programming development team. You can make communication on your team more efficient by just removing any dividing barriers between desks to allow people to talk easier. The ideal working environment is an open-plan area where desks and computers are arranged to make pair programming easier. The team should either use shared computers or their computers are set up with a consistent development environment so that that code can be worked on any machine with minimal disruption. Try to include a large area for daily stand-up meetings and add a conference table that gives the team a place to have more extensive group discussions.

To set your pace for a project, you need to take your iteration seriously. You want the most complete, tested, integrated, production-ready software you can get at each iteration. If your software is incomplete or riddled with defects, it is difficult to predict the amount of future effort required to release it. If you cannot get your tasks completed within a set iteration, you can have another iteration planning meeting to re-scope the iteration to maximize your velocity.

Even if you are very close to the end of the current iteration, it is best to get the entire team refocused on a single completed task than many incomplete tasks. Working lots of overtime sucks the life out of your team. When your team becomes tired and starts lacking motivation, they will get less work done, not more.

It is tough to make plans when your team does inconsistent amounts of work every month. Excessive overtime is very normally a result of bad planning and unrealistic goals. The purpose of your stand-up meeting is to get the whole team to communicate, so everyone knows what everyone else is doing.

A stand-up meeting every morning is used to communicate problems, solutions, and promote team focus. At a stand-up, everyone in the team should stand in a circle. By making the team stand you can avoid there being long conversations. It is more efficient to have one short meeting that everyone is required to attend than many meetings with few developers each. During a stand-up meeting, developers report at least three things. What was accomplished yesterday, what will be attempted today, and what problems are causing delays? The daily stand-up is probably one of the most valuable meetings your team can have to try and maintain momentum during an iteration as it encourages the team to bring issues out into the open, so the team can fix them together.

The project velocity is a measurement of how much work is getting done on your project each sprint. To measure the project's velocity, you simply add up the estimates of the user stories that were finished during the iteration. You also total up the estimates of tasks completed during the iteration. Both of these measurements are used for the iteration planning. During the iteration planning meeting, your customers or project sponsors are allowed to choose the same number of user stories equal to the project's velocity measured in the previous iteration. Those user stories are split down into tasks, and the team is allowed to assign the same number of tasks equal to the previous iterations project velocity.

This method for working our velocity allows developers to recover and clean up after a challenging iteration and helps to average out estimates in the future. Your project velocity will go up by letting a developer ask the customer for another story when their work is finished early, and no clean-up tasks remain. You should try to move people around in the team to avoid serious knowledge loss and coding bottlenecks. If any one person on your team can work in a given area, and that person leaves or just has too much work to do, you'll find that your project progress reduces to a crawl.

Cross-training is a crucial thing to consider in companies trying to avoid developers becoming islands of knowledge in certain technical areas. This can be a particular problem if a developer who is regarded as an "expert" in one area decides to leave the organization. Moving developers around in the code base in conjunction with pair programming does your cross-training for you. Instead of having one developer who is an expert for a particular piece of the system, everyone on that team will gain knowledge about the system as a whole.

The Extreme Programming methodology isn't perfect, and it won't fit for all organizations and teams. You should follow the XP rules to start with, but do not hesitate to change what doesn't work out. This isn't a free license to do whatever you want though. The rules have to be followed until the team, together, decides to change them.

Design

It is always easier to complete a simpler design than a complex one. Therefore, you should always strive to make your designs simple. It's always faster, simpler and less expensive to replace more complex code early before you waste a lot more time on it. A system metaphor is a story that everyone, including your customers, programmers, and managers can tell about how the system works. It's a naming concept for classes and methods that should make it easier for a team member to guess the functionality of a particular class or method from its name only.

A system metaphor should be helpful in figuring out the overall design of the system. The metaphor should also help the team find a common vocabulary, and the metaphor is useful when helping everyone reach agreements about our requirements.

When developers are faced with a problem they don't know the answer to straight away, create spike solutions to figure out the answer. A spike solution is a simple prototype to explore potential solutions and options. Build a spike only to address the particular problem being investigated and ignore all other concerns. Most spikes are designed to be throwaway prototypes that never make it into production, so you don't need to labor over their design.

The goal is reducing the risk of a technical problem or increase the reliability of the user story's estimate. If this is a particularly tough problem, you can also put two developers on it to try and solve the problem. You should aim to keep the system uncluttered with extra code that you think may be useful later on. It is always tempting to add functionality now rather than later because we see exactly how to add it or because it would make the system so much better. We need to continually remind ourselves that we are not going actually to need it.

Coding

Code must be formatted to agree with your team's coding standards. It's these coding standards that keep the code consistent and easy for the entire team to read and refactor. Code that looks the same also helps to encourage collective code ownership. It used to be quite common for a team to have a coding standards document that defined how the code should look, including the team's best practices for styling and formatting. The problem with this is that people rarely read them, let alone follow them. Nowadays it's much more common to use a developer productivity tool to guide the user to using best practices automatically.

Popular tools in use today, certainly from a .NET perspective are ReSharper from JetBrains, CodeRush from Dev Express, and JustCode from Telerik. These are all paid for solutions though. If you want to use a FREE alternative, then you can look at StyleCop for the .NET platform. Visual Studio also has its versions of some of these tools built in, but it is quite common to supplement Visual Studio with an additional add-on.

Other development platforms will have their variants of these tools, either separate additions to their development environments or built-in to their IDEs. These tools are so unbelievably powerful that it makes it frictionless to write code that conforms to a set of coding standards

When you create a unit test first before writing out your code, you'll find it much easier and faster to create the code. The time it takes to create a unit test and then create the code to make it pass is about the same time as just coding it out in the first instance.

Creating unit tests first helps the developer to consider what needs to be done and the system's requirements are firmly nailed down by the tests. There can be no misunderstanding the specification written in the form of executable code, and you'll also have immediate feedback during your work.

Under Extreme Programming, all code to be sent to production should be created by two people working together at a single computer. Pair programming will increase software quality without impacting the time to deliver. It can feel counter-intuitive at first, but two people working at a single computer will add as much functionality as two people working separately, except that it will be much higher in quality, and with increased code quality comes significant savings later in the project.

The best way to pair programming is just to sit side-by-side in front of the monitor and slide the keyboard backward and forwards between the two. Both programmers concentrate on the code being written.

Pair programming can sometimes be a difficult thing to sell to management as they just see two resources working on the same task at the double cost. They won't necessarily see that they are saving a lot of cost in the long run as the assumption is that code should be bug-free to start with.

Pair programming is a skill that takes time and effort to learn. Without force controlling the integration of code, developers test their code and integrate on their machines, believing all is well, but because of integration happening in parallel with other programming pairs, there can be combinations of source code which have not yet been tested together, which means integration problems can occur without detection. If ever there are problems and there is no clear-cut latest version of the entire source tree, this applies not only to the source code but to the unit test suite which must verify the source code's correctness.

If you cannot lay your hands on a complete, correct, and consistent test suite, you'll always be chasing bugs that may not exist and passing up on bugs that do. It is now standard practice to use some form of continuous integration system integrated with your source control repository. What this will do is when a developer checks in some code, the code is integrated with the main source code tree, built, and the tests are executed. If any part of this process fails, the development team will be notified immediately so that the issue can be resolved.

It's also common to have a source control system fail at check-in if the compile and test run fails. In Team Foundation Server, for example, this is called a gated build. Once you submit your code to the repository, the code is compiled on a build server, and the tests are executed. If this process fails for any reason, the developer would not be able to check-in their code. This process helps to ensure your code base is in a continual working state, and of high quality. Developers should be integrating and committing code into the source code repository at least every few hours or when they have written enough code to make their whole unit test pass. In any case, you should never hold onto changes for more than a day.

Continuous integration avoids diverging development, where developers are not communicating with each other about what can be reused or can be shared. Everyone on the team needs to work with the latest version of the source code, and changes to code should not be made to code that is out of date causing integration headaches. Each developer or pair of developers is responsible for integrating their code whenever a reasonable break presents itself.

A single machine dedicated to releases works well when the development team is co-located. This will be a build server that is controlled by checking commits from the source control repository like Team Foundation Server. This machine acts as a physical token to control release, and it also serves as an objective last word on what the common build contains. The latest combined unit test suite can be run before releasing when the code is integrated on the build machine, and because a single machine is used, the test suite is always up to date. If unit tests pass 100%, the changes are committed. If they fail for any reason, then the check-in is rejected, and the developers have to fix the problem.

Testing

Unit tests are one of the foundational cornerstones of Extreme Programming. First, you should decide on what unit testing framework you want to use. For .NET, for example, this might be NUnit or MSTest. Second, you should test all the classes in your system except trivial getters and setters, as those are usually omitted. You would also create your tests first before writing the actual application code. This doesn't mean you have to write all of the tests for the entire system up front, but before you tackle a new section, module or class, you would develop a set of tests as you go along with the coding.

While building up your tests and writing code to make the tests pass, you will, before you know it, have created a robust testing suite that can be executed over and over again. Unit tests are checked into the source code repository along with the code they test, and code without associated tests should not be released into production.

If a unit test is found to missing, then it should be created at that time and checked in. Usually, the biggest resistance to dedicating this amount of time to unit tests is a fast-approaching deadline, but during the life of a project, automated tests can save you hundreds of times the cost it takes to create them by finding and guarding against bugs.

Another common misconception is that a unit test can be written in the last few months of a project. Unfortunately, without unit tests, the development drags on and eats up those last few months of the project and then some. Even if the time is available, an excellent unit test suite takes time to evolve. Just having a suite of unit tests is meaningless if any of the tests fail for any reason. If you find a test as failing, you should fix it straight away and not continue coding until all the tests are passing. It doesn't matter if it's your test or someone else's but strive to get it fixed there and then.

If you have an automated continuous integration system setup, then you should be alerted straightaway if any of your tests start to fail. Even better, you'll be blocked from checking in the code if you have any check-in policies in force. When a bug is found, tests should be created to detect the bug and guard against it coming back. The debugging process also requires an acceptance test to be written to guard against it. Creating an acceptance test first before debugging helps customers concisely define the problem and communicate that problem to the programmers. Given a failed acceptance test, developers then start to create unit tests from a source-code-specific point of view.

Extreme Programming Diagram

Now that we have covered Extreme Programming in detail let's express some of what we have seen in an easy to understand diagram.

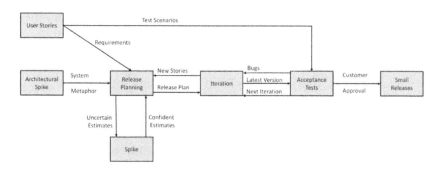

Extreme Programming (XP) Diagram

Here we have some of the different stages of XP, User Stories, Architectural Spikes, Release Planning, Development Spikes, Iterations, Acceptance Tests, and Small Releases. From the user story writing stage, we end up with a set of requirements and a series of test scenarios that form our acceptance tests.

From the architectural system spike, we end up with a system metaphor, which is a story that everyone, customers, programmers, and managers, can tell about how the system works. During the release planning phases, we determine what requirements are to be included in what releases, and when they should be released into. The developers and customers are both parts of this process.

If we are uncertain about particular estimates, we can create a spike application where a developer or developers spend a constrained amount of time to write a small example program to quickly solve the problem and therefore provide a more confident estimate.

The release plan then feeds into a development iteration where the code and unit tests are developed. Any new stories that come out during the iteration feedback into the release planning. From the iteration, you should have a working piece of software. This software should pass the acceptance tests set out from the user stories. If there are any bugs, then they are fixed by the developers.

There will typically be multiple iterations of a project. Once the acceptance tests pass from the iteration and the customer approves the system that has been developed in the iteration, a small release can take place at that point, which gives the users access to the real working code where they can start to reap the benefits early.

Scrum

In this chapter, we'll take a look at the Scrum methodology. Scrum is an iterative development framework where the value is delivered to the customer and users regularly. Scrum can be divided into three main areas:

- **Roles**—which contain the product owner, scrum master, and scrum team.
- **Ceremonies**—that contain the sprint planning, sprint review, and sprint retrospective ceremonies, and finally
- **Artefacts**—that contain product backlog, sprint backlog, and the release burn down chart.

First let's take a look at an overview of Scrum and its history.

Definition and History of Scrum

Scrum is an iterative and incremental agile software development framework for managing product development. It defines a flexible, holistic product development strategy where a development team works as a unit to reach a common goal. Scrum is a way to manage and organize a project, usually software development. In the Scrum world, instead of providing complete detailed descriptions that dictate how everything should be completed on a project, it is left up to the software development team to decide. This is because the team will know better how to solve the problem they are faced with.

Scrum encourages teams to be self-organizing and cross-functional where people are expected to be able to work in many areas and not just their personal niches. The Scrum team is self-organizing, in that there are no overall team leaders who decide which person will be doing which task and how the problem will be solved. Those are issues that are decided by the team as a whole.

Scrum was conceived by Ken Schwaber and Jeff Sutherland in the early 1990s. The term Scrum is borrowed heavily from the game of rugby to stress the importance of teams. Ken and Jeffs's paper showed that excellent performance in the development of new, complex products is achieved when teams, small self-organizing units of people, are given objectives instead of being handed tasks. Teams thrive when they are given objectives and a direction where they have room to make their own decisions on how to solve the objectives.

Teams require autonomy to achieve excellence. The Scrum framework for software development implements these principles described in this paper for developing and sustaining complex software projects. In February of 2001, Jeff and Ken were amongst 17 software development leaders who created a manifesto for agile software development.

Ken Schwaber, in 2002, founded the Scrum Alliance with Mike Cohn and Esther Derby, with Ken chairing the organization. In the following years, the highly successful certified scrum master programs were created and launched in 2006. Jeff Sutherland created his own company Scrum Inc, while still offering and teaching Scrum courses.

Ken left the Scrum Alliance in the fall of 2009 to found scrum.org to help improve the effectiveness of Scrum in the industry, mainly through their Scrum training. With the first publication of the Scrum Guide in 2010 and its incremental updates in 2011 and 2013, Jeff and Ken established a globally recognized body of knowledge of Scrum.

Overview of Scrum

Scrum is a project management framework that applies to any project with aggressive deadlines, complex requirements, and a degree of uniqueness. In Scrum, projects move forward by a series of iterations called sprints. Each sprint is typically 2-4 weeks in length. When describing the Scrum framework, it is easy to split it into three main areas. They are:

- **Roles**: which include the product owner, scrum master, and scrum team.

- **Ceremonies**: include the sprint planning meeting, sprint review, and sprint retrospective meetings

- **Scrum Artefacts**: and these include the product backlog, sprint backlog, and the burn down chart.

Let's first take a high-level look at these terms before we go into more detail. The product owner is a project's key stakeholder and represents the users for whom you are building the solution.

The product owner is a team member of the product management team or a key stakeholder or user of the system. It is quite common for a business analyst with domain experience to take on the product owner role for the development team who will regularly engage with the customers.

The scrum master is responsible for making sure the team is as productive as possible. The scrum master does this by helping teams use the scrum process by removing impediments to progress, by protecting the team from the outside, and so on. Their role is very much facilitating the team to steer their product to completion, and they act very much as a servant leader fulfilling the needs of the team. The typical scrum team has between five and nine people. A scrum project can easily scale into the hundreds. However, scrum can easily be used by 1-person teams, and often is.

This team does not include any of the normal software development roles such as developer, designer, architect, or tester. Everyone on the product works together as a team to complete a set of work they are collectively committed to complete within a sprint. Scrum teams tend to develop a deep form of camaraderie and a feeling that we're all in this together. At the start of a sprint, there is a sprint planning meeting that is held. During this meeting, the product owner presents the top items on the product backlog to the team. The scrum team then selects what they can complete during the coming sprint. That selected work is then moved from the product backlog to a sprint backlog, which is a list of tasks needed to complete the product backlog items the team has committed to finishing in the sprint.

At the end of each sprint, the team will demo the completed functionality from that sprints goal at the sprint review meeting, during which the team shows what they have accomplished during the sprint. Typically, this takes the form of demonstration of new features, but in an informal way. This meeting doesn't need to be very long or onerous to the development team but is a good forum to demonstrate the work completed in the sprint. Also at the end of each sprint, the team conducts a sprint retrospective, which is a meeting where the team, including the scrum master and product owner, will reflect on how well the Scrum process is working for them, and what changes they may wish to make for it to work even better.

Each day there is a meeting between the entire team called the stand-up. This meeting helps set the context for each day's work and helps the team stay on track. All team members have to attend the daily scrum. Ideally, everyone in the team stands in a circle. Everyone is made to stand so that their update is brief; otherwise, it can become uncomfortable. The team needs to answer three questions.

- What did I achieve yesterday?

- What do I plan to achieve today?

- Is there anything that is blocking me?

The product backlog is a prioritized list of features containing every desired feature or change in a product. There are multiple types of backlog in Scrum, the product backlog is a list of the desired features for the product, and a sprint backlog is a list of tasks to be completed within that sprint.

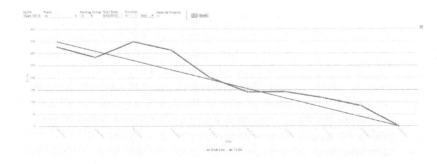

Example Burn down chart

On a Scrum project, the team will track its progress against a release plan on the burndown chart, as you can see in Figure 5. The burndown chart is updated at the end of each sprint by the scrum master. The horizontal axis of the chart shows the date and the vertical axis illustrates the amount of work remaining at the start of the sprint. Work remaining can be displayed in whatever unit the team prefers. This could be story points, ideal days or team days. Before we look at the Roles, Ceremonies, and Artefacts in more detail, let's look at a visual representation of the Scrum process.

Visualizing Scrum

The product backlog is a feature list that is prioritized and contains every desired feature or change to the product. When you have a sprint planning meeting, backlog items from the product backlog are selected to be implemented in the next sprint and placed into the sprint backlog. Once the sprint backlog has been identified from the product backlog, the team enters a 2-4-week sprint where they implement the items in the sprint backlog.

The Scrum Development Process

Each day during the sprint, a brief meeting called a daily scrum is conducted. This meeting helps set the context for each day's work and helps the team stay on track. All the team members are required to attend the daily scrum. At the end of the sprint, the team should have a potentially shippable product that could go into production and give value to the end user. Now that we've had an overview of the scrum let's look at each of the roles, artifacts, and ceremonies in detail.

Scrum Roles

Scrum defines three main Roles:

- Product Owner

- Scrum Master

- Scrum Team

Usually, the Scrum team's product owner is the project's key stakeholder, but it could also be a business analyst who works closely with the business and the users of the system. Part of the product owner's responsibility is to have the vision of what he or she wishes to build and convey that vision to the rest of the scrum team.

The product owner is key to successfully starting any agile software development project. The product owner works by maintaining the product backlog, which is a prioritized feature list for the product.

The product owner is usually a user of the system or someone from Marketing, Product Management, or anyone with an understanding of the users, the marketplace, the competition, and the future trends for the domain or type of system being developed. This could also be a business analyst who has an excellent grasp of the business domain. The product owner prioritizes the product backlog during the sprint planning meeting.

It is the development team that selects the amount of work that they feel they can complete each sprint and how many sprints it will take to complete their objectives. It is not the responsibility of the product owner to tell the development team how much work they should do in a sprint or how many sprints are required to complete the work. This should come from the rest of the development team who will be doing the actual estimates. Requirements are allowed to change within Scrum, and this change is encouraged, but these changes should come outside the sprint and ready for the next sprint planning meeting. Once a team starts on a sprint, it should remain focused entirely on delivering the work for that sprint.

The product owner's role requires a person with particular sets of skills, including availability to the team, business and domain expertise, and excellent communication skills. It is essential that the product owner is available to his or her team all the time, and that they should be committed to doing whatever is necessary to build the best product.

Business and domain knowledge is important for agile product owners because he or she is the decision-maker regarding what features the product will have. That means a product owner should understand the market, the customer, and the business, to make the right decisions. Communication is a huge part of the product owner's role and responsibilities.

The product owner role requires working closely with the key stakeholders throughout the organization, so they must be able to communicate different messages to different people on the team about the product at any given time. The scrum master is responsible for making sure the Scrum team lives by the values and practices of Scrum.

The scrum masters' role is like that of a coach for the team, helping the team do the best work they possibly can. This involves removing any impediments or blockers to progress, facilitating meetings, and doing things like working with the product owner to make sure the product backlog is in good shape and ready for the next sprint. The scrum master role is commonly filled by a former project manager or a technical team leader, but it can be anyone.

People who are new to the scrum master role sometimes struggle with the apparent contradiction of the scrum master, who is both servant leader to the team and also someone with no authority as a team leader or manager. This contradiction disappears when we realize that although the scrum master has no power over scrum team members directly, the scrum master does have authority over the process.

The scrum master is there to help the team in its use of Scrum. They're a bit like a personal trainer who helps you stick with an exercise workout. A good personal trainer will motivate you, while at the same time making sure you don't cheat by skipping the hard exercise.

A personal trainer cannot make you do any exercise you don't want to. Instead, the trainer reminds you of your goals and how you've chosen to meet them. To the extent that the trainer does have the authority that has been granted by the client, scrum masters are much the same. They have authority, but the authority is granted to them by the team.

The scrum master can say to the team, look, we're supposed to deliver potentially shippable software at the end of each sprint. We didn't do it this time. What we can do is make sure we do better on the next sprint. This is the scrum master exerting authority over the process. Something has gone wrong with the process if the team has failed to deliver something potentially shippable. But because the scrum master's authority does not extend beyond the process, the same scrum master should not say "because we failed to deliver some something potentially shippable last sprint, I want Kevin to review all the code before it gets checked in."

Having Kevin review the code might be a good idea, but the decision is not the scrum masters to make. With power limited to ensuring the team follows a process, the scrum master's role can be more challenging than that of a typical manager.

Project managers often have the fallback position of "do it because I say so." The times when a scrum master can say that are limited and restricted to ensuring that scrum is being followed.

In a Scrum team environment, you don't have fixed roles and responsibilities, like front-end developer, back-end developer, database engineer, tester, etc. Everyone on the project works together to complete an agreed set of product objectives they've collectively committed to complete within the sprint. Because of this cross-discipline nature, scrum teams develop a sincere form of team spirit and feel like we're all in this together.

Scrum Ceremonies

In Scrum, there are four ceremonies that the scrum team will be involved with. These are the:

- Sprint planning meeting
- Sprint review meeting
- Sprint retrospective
- Daily scrum

The sprint planning meeting is attended by the scrum master, product owner, and the rest of the scrum team including developers, testers, architects and business analysts. Outside stakeholders and users may attend if they are invited along by the team, but generally, they won't be attending this meeting. During the sprint planning meeting, the product owner describes the highest priority features to the team. The team should then ask enough questions, so they can turn a high-level user story of the product backlog into a more detailed set of tasks for the sprint backlog.

The product owner doesn't have to describe every item being tracked in the product backlog. A good rule of thumb is for the product owner to attend this meeting with enough work to talk about to fill up two sprints. This means that if the team is likely to finish what they thought they would get done in one sprint, the product owner is prepared with details of additional work and priorities.

By the end of each sprint, you are required to deliver a potentially shippable product. This means that at the end of each sprint the team has to produce a coded, tested, and usable piece of software. A sprint review meeting is held at the end of each sprint, and during this meeting, the scrum team shows what they have accomplished during the sprint as a live demo of the features.

This meeting should be quite brief and not take up too much of everyone's time, as it'll also be attended by product customers and management whose time can be limited.

Participants in the sprint review typically include the product owner, the scrum team, the scrum master, management, customers, and developers from other products. During the sprint review, the product is assessed against the original sprint goal. Ideally, the team has completed each product backlog item brought into the sprint, but it's more important that they achieve the overall goal of the sprint. No matter how good a scrum team is, there is always the opportunity to improve.

Although a good team will always be looking for improvement opportunities, the team should set aside a brief dedicated period at the end of each sprint to reflect on how they are doing and find ways to improve. This takes place during the sprint retrospective meeting. The Retrospective is normally the last thing to be done in a sprint, and the whole team, including both the product owner and scrum master, should participate. A retrospective meeting should last for around an hour. However, occasionally a controversial topic will come up, or a team conflict will escalate, and a Retrospective could take longer.

During a retrospective meeting, the team should answer the following questions.

- What should we start doing?
- What should we stop doing?
- What should we continue doing?

The scrum master can run the sprint retrospective meeting by asking everyone just to shout out and contribute ideas. The scrum master can go around each person in the room asking them to identify anything to start, stop or continue.

After an initial list of ideas has been thought through, teams will vote on specific items to focus on during the next sprint.

The daily scrum meeting is held every day, preferably in the morning. This meeting is crucial as it allows the team to understand where everyone else is within the sprint. Everyone stands in a circle during the meeting. By making everyone stand up, it ensures that their updates are brief, as standing up for too long is uncomfortable. The team has to answer three questions.

- What did you achieve yesterday?
- What will you achieve today?
- Is there anything blocking you?

If anything is blocking you, then you can work with the scrum master to resolve the blocking issue to enable you to continue.

Scrum Artifacts

As part of the Scrum process, there are three main artifacts you will use besides the actual delivered product. These are the:

- Product backlog
- Sprint backlog
- Burn down chart

In Scrum, the product backlog is a prioritized list of features containing short descriptions of all the desired functionality in the product. When using Scrum, it's not necessary to start a product with a long upfront effort to document all the requirements as you would in Waterfall.

Typically, a scrum team and its product owners will begin by writing down everything that they can think of for the backlog prioritization. This product backlog usually is always more than enough for the first sprint.

The scrum product backlog is then allowed to grow and change as more is learned about the product and its customers. A typical scrum backlog comprises the following different types of items:

- Features
- Bugs
- Technical work
- Knowledge acquisition

The main way for a scrum team to express features on the product backlog is by writing user stories. User stories are short, simple descriptions of the desired functionality told from the perspective of the user. An example would be, "as a pharmacist, I can dispense products from a customer's prescription, which then appear on the customers dispense items record."

There's also no difference between a bug and a new feature. Each describes something different that the user wants, so bugs are also put into the product backlog.

Technical implementation work and technical spike activities also belong in the backlog. An example of technical work would be, upgrade all developers' workstations to Windows 10, or migrate to using a continuous integration server for continuous delivery.

An example of technical spike work could be a backlog item about researching various JavaScript libraries and then making a technical decision. This may result in a small piece of work to solidify this knowledge.

The product owner shows up at the sprint planning meeting with a prioritized product backlog and describes the top items to the team. The team will then determine which items they can realistically complete during the next sprint. The team then moves items from the product backlog to the sprint backlog. In doing this, they expand each product backlog item into one or more sprint backlog tasks, so they can more effectively share work during the next sprint.

The sprint backlog is a list of tasks that are identified by the scrum master to be completed during the next sprint. During the planning meeting, the team works together to select some product backlog items to work on and identifies the tasks necessary to complete each story. Most teams also estimate how many hours each task will take for someone on the team to complete, although time-based estimates are almost always inaccurate. The reason for this is because each person will have different abilities and it will take them a different amount of time, based on experience, to complete the tasks. It is much better to estimate relative complexity and effort instead by using a Fibonacci number sequence or t-shirt sizes. A small t-shirt size might be equivalent to putting a field on the website and then persisting it to the database, and then everything else is estimated based on that relative complexity.

It's essential that the team selects the items and the size of the sprint backlog. Because other people are committing to completing the tasks, they must be the people to choose what they are committing to during the sprint.

The sprint backlog can be maintained as a spreadsheet, but it's also possible to use your bug tracking system or any number of software products designed specifically for Scrum or Agile. Team Foundation Server with the Scrum template, Jira, and VersionONE are common options to choose from.

Team members, during the sprint, are expected to update the sprint backlog as new information is available, but minimally once per day. Many teams will do this during the daily scrum. Once a day the estimated work remaining in the sprint is calculated and graphed by the scrum master, resulting in a sprint burndown chart.

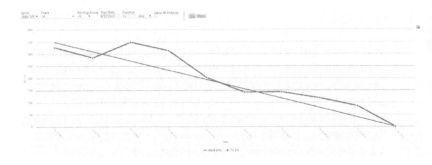

Example Burn down chart

The team will do as best as it can to move the right amount of work into a sprint, but sometimes too much or too little work is taken in during the planning. In this case, the team needs to add or move new tasks. On a Scrum project, the team tracks its progress against a release plan on a release burndown chart.

The release burndown chart is published at the end of each sprint by the scrum master. The horizontal axis of the burndown chart shows the sprints, and the vertical axis indicates the amount of work remaining at the start of each sprint. Work remaining can be shown in whatever unit the team prefers, story points, ideal days or team days.

The burndown chart is an essential part of any agile project, and it is a way for the team to see what is happening and how progress is being made during each sprint.

One issue that may be noticed in the burndown chart is whether or not the actual work line is above or below the ideal work line, and this depends on how accurate the original estimates were. This means if your team keeps on overestimating their time required, the progress will always appear ahead of schedule. If they consistently underestimate the time required, they will always look on schedule.

Extreme Programming vs. Scrum

Now that we have taken a look at both Extreme Programming and Scrum let's take a look at some of the main differences between the two. Scrum teams work in iterations which are called sprints, and these sprints are generally between two and four weeks in length, although nothing is stopping you from having a one-week sprint if you have a small team.

Having such a short sprint can be problematic, though, if you have to fit in planning meetings, sprint reviews, and retrospectives all into one week. Extreme Programming teams work in iterations, and these iterations are 1-2 weeks in length. Once a sprint has started under Scrum, the scrum team doesn't allow any changes to that sprint until they are finished.

The team will continue as planned to the end of the sprint, and then do any pre-planning as necessary for the next sprint. With Extreme Programming, teams are much more amenable to change in their iteration. If a change is required, the team will hold another planning session and adjust their iteration accordingly. In Scrum, the product owner prioritizes the product backlog, but the team determines the sequence in which they will develop the backlog items.

The team is trusted and expected to set their own pace and workload within the sprint. The backlog will be prioritized, which causes the team to work on the high-value items first, but the team picks the order for these high-value items to be implemented.

In Extreme Programming, the teams work in a strict priority order as set out in the planning sessions and tend not to deviate from that order. Scrum does not prescribe any engineering practices for the developers, as it is more of a lightweight project management framework. Extreme Programming, on the other hand, is a very engineering-based methodology that defines many engineering practices like test-driven development, pair programming, and continuous integration.

Extreme Programming comes with many rules that can be hard for new teams to adopt. In my experience, what tends to happen is teams adopt scrum, as it is a lightweight framework for managing your agile project, and then introduces different engineering practices from Extreme Programming as deemed necessary. For example, at the time of writing this book, I am working on a scrum team where we do test-drive development and continuous integration and delivery.

Lean Software Development

Lean Software Introduction

This book is split into six main chapters. In this first section, we will take a look at the outline for the rest of the book and also introduce a fictional company that we will use as an example throughout the remainder of the book.

We will start off by looking at the history of Lean Manufacturing. Lean is not a new concept that was designed for software development. It has firm roots in manufacturing, and we will take a look at this background before talking about software development.

Then we will look at how Lean can be applied to software development. Lean software development was coined by Mary and Tom Poppendieck who are 2 IT Developers and Leaders who have applied the Lean Manufacturing concepts to the software development world. This chapter will talk about Lean Software Developments 7 principles which are:

- Eliminate Waste

- Amplify Learning

- Decide as Late as Possible

- Deliver as Fast as Possible

- Empower the Team

- Build Quality / Integrity in?

- See the Whole

Once we have looked at the seven principles in Lean Software Development, we'll then look at both Agile and Lean being used together. We will answer the question, should you use Agile or Lean? This is a question that comes up frequently when people are first exploring lean, and this chapter will help provide an answer.

Next, we will look at different practices you should adopt to that will help you to be leaner. This will include such practices as:

- Source Control

- Automated Testing

- Continuous Integration

Once we have explored these different practices, we will then look at Kanban. Kanban is a task and workflow tracking method for managing work with a focus on just-in-time delivery while at the same time not overloading the team members. In this approach, the process from the definition of a task to its delivery to the customer is displayed for participants to see.

This chapter will explore Kanban in some detail as it is a perfect technique for running a lean team. The key concept explored is that work is pulled from work queues and not pushed. The idea is to limit the amount of work in progress at any one time. The idea is that if you limit work in progress, you will get more work done.

It might be useful for you to have an understanding of Agile, Scrum, and Extreme Programming before reading this book. It's not essential, but it might help with giving you a fully rounded view of different ways of running a software project.

Our Fictional Company

As we explore Lean software development, I will use a fictional company to apply some of the ideas. Our fictional company is a financial services software provider called Deltasoft. Deltasoft has three development teams. They used to be a very waterfall-based company, but a couple of years ago they moved over to being more agile and adopted Scrum as their software development methodology.

One of their development teams has recently finished work on a debt management application, and they are about to start work on a contact center call, handling system that integrates with their loan management system.

The team consists of a

- Development Manager called Steve

- Development Manager called **John**

- 5 Developers, **Phil, Peter, Sarah, Hitesh, Oliver**

- 2 Testers who are both manual testers and Automation testers, **Douglas, Amanda**

- 1 Scrum Master called **Scott**, who makes sure the team follows the Scrum process and manages the product backlog, stand-ups, planning sessions and retrospectives.

- And finally, 1 Product Owner and Business analyst called **Sam**.

I will refer to this fictional team as we progress through the remainder of this book to demonstrate some of the Lean practices. Let's now proceed to the next chapter and take a look at Lean manufacturing.

Lean Manufacturing

In this chapter, we will take a look at the background of Lean with Lean Manufacturing as this is where the Lean Software Development movement grew up from. In this chapter, we will first look at the history of Lean starting with Henry Ford and then the Toyota Production System. We will then take a look at Just in Time manufacturing, Automation, Waste and Lean Process. This will give you the necessary background and context before we look at Lean Software Development.

Let's start off with a brief history of Lean.

History of Lean Manufacturing

Henry Ford and the Model-T

Henry Ford of the Ford Motor Company was one of the first people to introduce the concepts of Lean Manufacturing. Henry Ford used the notion of "continuous flow" on the production assembly line for his Model T car. On the production line, he kept manufacturing standards very tight. This meant that each stage of the manufacturing process worked together with each other step. This resulted in little waste.

But Ford's process wasn't flexible. His assembly lines produced the same thing, again and again, and the process didn't easily allow for any modifications or changes to the end product. This product line produced only 1 product, the Model-T car.

The process adopted by Henry Ford was called a "push" process. This meant he defined the level of production instead to determine how many cars are manufactured each day. The opposite of this is called a "pull" process which is led by consumer demand instead of defining a fixed level of output.

By defining a fixed level of output, this led to significant inventories of unsold cars being stored. This lead to lots of wasted money in held stock sitting idle. Other manufacturers began to use Ford's ideas, but many realized that the inflexibility of his system was a problem.

The system in place at Ford would create a significant buffer of inventory being stored in warehouses. This may seem like a good thing to ensure you have a product ready for customers, but it can cause you big problems. If you hold a lot of items in inventory, you're locking away a vast amount of cash unnecessarily. These items can be lost, stolen, or damaged, or they can deteriorate, and as you can imagine, holding lots of stock of cars takes up a lot of space. Your products can become obsolete, mainly when products are improved or changed, and this leaves you with a huge inventory of outdated stock that needs to either be sold at a reduced cost which can cause a financial loss or scrapped which will result in a much more significant loss.

The Toyota Production System

In 1945, in post-war Japan, the president of Toyota Motor Company, Kiichiro Toyoda, hinted that the Japanese car industry would die if it did not catch up with America within three years. This proved to be incorrect as the industry recovered, but it did motivate the creation of the Toyota Production System by Taiichi Ohno, a Japanese industrial engineer, and businessman.

In the 1950s, a team from Toyota visited some American businesses to look at their manufacturing processes. One of the companies they visited was Ford, but they were not impressed with what they found due to the amount of spare inventory being held by Ford. What did impress the Japanese team though was when they visited some American supermarkets as they were impressed with the way products are restocked after being purchased by customers. This method of working is what inspired Taiichi Ohno to create the Just in Time system that aims to keep inventories low at each manufacturing stage.

Inventory is a waste that costs money, and it hides problems in the production system; this includes issues such as inadequate capacity, inflexible and unreliable equipment. When items are ready just in time, they are not just sitting around idle and taking up space in a warehouse. This means that they don't cost you anything to hold onto them, and they're not becoming obsolete or deteriorating on the shelves. However, for this to work efficiently, without the buffer of having items in stock, you must tightly control your manufacturing process so that parts are ready when you need them. When you do control the manufacturing process, you can be very responsive to customer orders.

The key benefits of JIT are:

- Low inventory

- Low wastage

- High quality production

- High customer responsiveness

Automation

Automation is an essential factor in Lean manufacturing systems. It describes machines that automate a process but are also smart enough to know when something is going wrong and stop the system immediately. This kind of machine can run unattended and still provide workers with the confidence that it is working without issue. When the machine detects an error condition, it should stop, and a human worker will stop the manufacturing line. This focuses everyone's attention on finding the cause of the problem and fixing it so that it will not recur.

Types of Waste

Lean manufacturing has strict views on waste. Shigeo Shingo, a world-leading expert on manufacturing and the Toyota Production System, defined seven types of waste that can be remembered using the acronym DOTWIMP:

Defects: This is perhaps the most obvious type of waste. Lean focuses on preventing defects instead of the traditional "find and fix" mentality.

Overproduction: Producing more inventory than is required or manufacturing it before it is needed.

Transportation: The unnecessary transport of parts and inventory between manufacturing stages. When you move material and parts between factories, work cells, desks, or machines, no value is created.

Waiting: People, inventory or parts waiting for the next step in production.

Inventory: All materials whether work-in-progress or finished products that are not being actively processed. Any stored inventory that is not directly needed now requires storage and is therefore waste.

Motion: If your staff on the production line or your inventory and stock has to move between buildings, then this extra movement is a waste due to the accumulated transportation time required.

Processing: Over-processing beyond the standard required by the customer. This adds additional cost without adding extra value.

There is also an additional eighth waste that is commonly used outside of the standard DOTWIMP version.

Underutilization of People: This is often cited as an additional type of waste beyond the original seven, and it refers to the underutilization of the worker's creativity and resourcefulness.

Lean Principles

Taiichi Ohno started with Just-In-Time and automation which are the two central tenants of the Toyota Production System. Lean in the modern-day focuses on five core principles and many other practices that have been influenced by the Toyota production system. The five principles are Value, Value Stream, Flow, Pull, and Perfection. Let's take a quick look at each of these.

Value: The first principle is Value that is defined by your customers or users. What does the customer value in the product? It is essential to learn what is classed as value or not, from your customers perspective. Understanding this value helps you map out a value stream.

Value stream: Once you know what the customer values in your product, you can create a value stream map. The value stream map helps you to identify the series of steps needed to develop your product. Each step is classed as either value-added, non-value-added but necessary, or non-value-added waste. We will look in more detail at value stream mapping in the next chapter when we dive more into Lean Software Development.

Flow: The production process must be designed to flow continuously. If the value chain stops moving forward (for any reason), then waste is occurring.

Pull: Let customer orders pull product or value. This pulls ripples back through the entire value stream and makes sure that nothing is manufactured before it is required, therefore eliminating most in-process inventory.

Perfection: You must always aim for perfection by continually identifying and removing waste from your manufacturing process.

Kaizen - Continuous Improvement

Kaizen is a Japanese word for "improvement." When this is used in a business context and applied to the workplace, kaizen refers to continuously improving all aspects of that business and involves all employees from the CEO to the individual manufacturing workers.

The primary purpose of Kaizen is to eliminate waste in your manufacturing process. Japanese businesses first introduced kaizen after World War 2 and after being partly influenced by American companies. Since then, it has spread around the world and also implemented in areas outside business and manufacturing.

The Kaizen process suggests a human approach to workers and increasing productivity:

"The idea is to nurture the company's people as much as it is to praise and encourage participation in kaizen activities."

Successful implementation requires

"the participation of workers in the improvement."

People at all levels of a company should participate in doing kaizen. This starts from the CEO and flows down to all other staff. Kaizen is commonly associated with companies such as Toyota, but it has also implemented in non-manufacturing environments.

There are two popular techniques used to assist Kaizen. These are PDCA, which stands for Plan Do Check Act, and the 5 Why's method.

Plan, Do, Check, Act

Plan–Do–Check–Act is a four-step method used in business for the control and continuous improvement of processes and products. It is also commonly referred to as the Deming cycle. Another version of this PDCA cycle is OPDCA. The added "O" stands for observation or as some versions say, "Grasp the current condition." This emphasis on observation and current condition has currency with Lean manufacturing/Toyota Production System literature.

PLAN: Plan the steps necessary to deliver results for your stated goals. When possible, you start on a small scale to test potential effects.

DO: Implement the plan for stage one and collect data for charting and analysis in the following "CHECK" and "ACT" steps.

CHECK: Study the results from the 'DO" step and compares the results against the expected results in the "PLAN" stage. Use any results observed to come up with a plan to improve your process.

ACT: Implement the plan from the previous "CHECK" stage to improve your processes. Once these have been implemented, they become the new baseline for you to start the whole PDCA process again to find further refinements.

5 Why's

5 Whys is a technique used to explore the cause and effect relationships underlying a particular problem. The goal is to determine the cause of a defect or problem by repeating the question "Why?" 5 times. Each question forms the basis of the next question.

Sakichi Toyoda developed the 5 Whys technique, and the Toyota Motor Corporation used it during the evolution of its manufacturing methodologies. It is not always possible to find a single root-cause of a problem as there could be multiple causes. To unearth various root-causes, you repeat the five whys technique by asking different questions each time.

Lean Software Development

In this chapter, we will first look at where Lean Software Development came from and then we will look at the 7 principles that underpin Lean Software Development.

At a high level, they are:

Eliminate waste: This is where you should only spend time on what adds real customer value.

Amplify learning: This is when you have tough problems, you increase feedback.

Decide as late as possible: This is about keeping your options open as long as practical, but no longer.

Deliver as fast as possible: This is about delivering value to customers as soon as they ask for it.

Empower the team: This is letting the people who add value to your customers use their full potential.

Build integrity in: This is about not trying to tack on integrity and monitoring after the fact but building it in from the start. And finally.

Seeing the whole: This is where you should beware of the temptation to optimize parts of the system at the expense of the whole.

We will first go through all the theory which will give you a great understanding of all these principles and then we will apply them to our fictional company Deltasoft.

The Origins of Lean Software Development

The term Lean Software Development was originally talked about in a book by the same name, written by Mary Poppendieck and Tom Poppendieck.

Lean Software Development - An Agile Toolkit

The book teaches a modified form of lean that is more applicable to software development. The book also features a set of 22 tools and compares the tools to agile practices.

I recommend reading this book if you are interested in the concepts of Lean Software Development as it supplements this book very well if you want to delve into the subject in greater detail. This book takes a higher-level look at lean to enable you to acquire skills quickly, but the book by Mary and Tom goes into extreme detail on each principle, much more than would make sense for this introductory book. So, once you have finished this book, please do check out their book once you have a firm grasp of lean.

Let's take a look at the 7 principles of Lean Software Development.

Lean Software Development Principles

Eliminate waste

The lean movement regards anything not adding value to the customer as waste. To eliminate waste, first, you need to be able to recognize it. Extra processes like paperwork and software features not often used by customers are regarded as waste. Switching developers between tasks frequently are waste. Waiting for other teams or processes to complete is waste. Defects and lower quality implementations are also waste.

Let's explore some of these wastes in more detail.

Defects

Defects are anything in your code and system that is not working as expected. Defects cause expensive rework and the time of a tester or QA engineer to find the defect in the first place. This time in finding the flaws is a non-value-added waste. Your focus when working towards being leaner is to prevent mistakes in the first place with the proper unit and integration testing, whereas in more traditional software development, the emphasis has always been on finding the defect after the fact.

When defects have been found, it is essential to get to a root cause of why the defect occurs and ensure that the team learns from it so that it doesn't happen again. Detecting defects immediately through unit testing is much less waste than a defect going unfound for a few weeks as the code in question should still be very fresh in a developer's mind, and they can fix it easier than when it is found a lot later. The biggest waste here is if a defect makes it through into production and causes the customer a problem.

Handoffs

For anyone that has worked on a large waterfall project before, the concept of handoffs will be familiar. You might be familiar with something like the following.

1. A business analyst writes up a large requirement design document. This is then handed off to solution designers to perform a system design.

2. Once the solution designers have done a complete system design, they then hand off the design to the development team.

3. The development team write the code and then hand off to the QA team.

In each handoff stage, there is a lot of knowledge that is lost through the handoff as it is not possible to record every bit of information that has been discovered. This means that by the time the developers write the code, the gap in their knowledge to that of the business analysts can be quite large. Therefore, if you want to limit this knowledge loss waste, you should avoid formal handoffs between teams.

This is why with Agile and Scrum, they advocate each role being a part of the project team, sitting and working closely together. This tight-knit team working, and collaboration helps to ensure that knowledge is shared across the team.

Partially Completed Work

Next, we have partially completed work. This is any code that has been started but not finished. By not completing, we don't just mean code that is left uncompleted. The developer can technically complete the code, but it is not unit tested. So, what is complete? For any work to be considered complete, it should be deployed into production and generating value and benefit for the end user.

Code that is not complete and just left to linger can potentially become obsolete, and you never have any idea if it will work or not. If your code is never used, like a project you have already paid for that code to be written, but if it never makes it into a user's hands, then that system will not start paying back which makes it a sunk cost. This type of sunk cost is one of the worst kinds of waste as it is costing actual money which is being thrown away.

Delays

Any delay on a project is considered waste. For example, if a member of the team has to seek answers to a question, if the people they need to talk to are not available straight away then a delay is caused, and this creates waste. Without getting this correct answer straight away, the team member may be forced to switch to another task, guess the response and risk doing rework, or trying to research the answer themselves which may take up valuable time and still result in the wrong answer.

Extra Features

The next waste we have is that of extra features. As developers, it is very tempting to add lots of features to solve all know scenarios in a software solution but adding in additional features is also a waste as that code needs to be tested and maintained even if it is not directly bringing any value to your end customer.

Every line of code that is added to a system increases the complexity and adds a potential failure point, so you should only add code that is necessary to satisfy your customers' requirements. If any code is not needed now, then putting it into your system should be considered a waste.

Task Switching

The next waste we have is that of task switching. One of the most significant disruptions you can do to a software developer is to have them switch tasks. Task switching requires a lot of mental shifting from one train of thought to another. It takes time for a developer to focus their brain on a task to be effective at problem-solving. Switching to another task before they are ready to restart the process of them getting started.

If you need a developer to work on two tasks, the fastest way for them to achieve this is to concentrate on one at a time. Complete the first task and then move onto the second. If they flit between the two tasks, it will take them longer to complete the work.

Unneeded Processes

The final waste we will look at is an unneeded process. Have you ever worked for an organization where you have to go through a very lengthy process to just get some simple software changes deployed? I have many times, and it is painful. I used to work for a large healthcare provider, and we needed to implement a small data change that just added two rows to a database table.

As you can imagine this was a straightforward SQL script that was first tested in a test environment. The process to get this deployed involved a developer having to write deployment and rollback instructions, and a QA engineer writing a test report. I then had to go into a change management system and raise a change request that had a 3-day lead time and required five people to sign off the change. I had to chase every one of these five people to get their approval before the change was due to start.

This small and very low-risk change had to go through the same process that a huge high-risk change would. It involved my time, a developer and QA engineer, and then finally the time of an engineer who had to be booked to run the script in production. This seemingly simple change required a lot of time and resources. This was incredibly wasteful.

In heavily regulated environments a strict change control process might be required, but the process should be suitable to the complexity and risk of the change. In my example it wasn't, even for a very low-risk change, we had to use the same process that a major high-risk change would go through.

In Mary and Tom Poppendiecks book, Lean Software Development is an Agile Toolkit; they mention that if you do have to carry out paperwork that adds little customer value, there are three rules you should remember:

"Keep it short. Keep it high level. Do it offline."

Now that we have looked at some examples of waste in software development let's look at a technique for helping to detect waste in the system you are building. Let's take a look at Value Stream Maps.

Eliminate Waste - Value Stream Maps

A value stream map is a visual representation of all the steps in a process from start to finish. Each step in the value stream map contains data that describes the actual work time where the value is being generated and any waiting time, where waiting equals waste. You identify each step as value added, non-value added, or non-value added but necessary.

By visually mapping out these processes with work and wait for the times you can easily spot bottlenecks in a process and any steps that are just not added any value. This gives you the starting foundations to start optimizing that process. We will look more closely later in this book at Value Stream Mapping with our fictional company Deltasoft.

Value vs Non Value	Results
Cycle Time	250 days
Value Add Days	105 days
Non Value Add Days	145 days
Efficiency %	105 / 250 = 42%

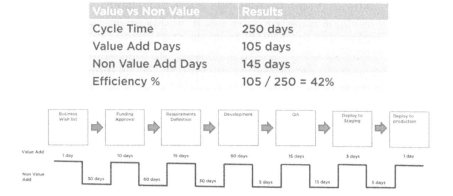

Example value stream map

Let's look at a simple example of a value stream map. On the diagram above, in the boxes, you can see the stages of a process. This process describes a wish list coming in from the business which then requires funding approval. Once funding is approved, the business analysts can define the requirements which are then handed off to the development team. Once the code is developed, the QA team test the code, and it is then deployed to a staging environment and then production.

Yes, I know, this is so waterfall that you can hear the water crashing over the rocks but bear with me. Let's now look at the value-add verses non-value-add timings. The alternating lines at the bottom of the diagram show value added time on the top and no value-added time on the bottom. Value added is the time that is being well spent towards providing value to the customer and non-value-added time is the time that is waste.

Let's go from left to right and see what is going on. This is based on a real example of a company I have worked at before, so it's not a made-up scenario.

First of all, the business comes up with a wish list. This takes about a day of effort. Then there is a 30-day delay before the funding approval stage starts. This takes about 10 days in total of meetings and justifications. Once funding is approved, there is a 60-day delay before it makes it to the project team, to start their work. The business analysts take 15 days to do their research and produce a requirements document. This is then handed over to developers who have a 30-day delay before they can start working on the features. Their development takes 60 days in total, and this is the value add time as they are developing the actual solution for the customer.

Once they have completed development, there is a 5-day delay before QA picks up the code and performs 15 days of testing. This could include functional, non-functional and performance testing. Once QA signs off the features, there is a 15-day delay while the relevant paperwork is filled in for a release and the appropriate teams are lined up for the deployment. The deployment to staging takes three days and then five days later the features are deployed to production. This is just one example; you could then produce a value stream map for each of those stages to start investigating waste at each stage.

The time from when the customer comes up with their wish list to it being delivered into production, so they can start realizing benefits from it is 250 days in total. This is called the cycle time. That's 105 days of actual value-add time and 145 days of non-value-added time. If we want to calculate the efficiency of this value stream, we'll divide the value-add amount of 105 days by the total cycle time of 250 days. This gives us an efficiency score of 42%.

Creating a value stream map is a paper and pencil exercise you can quickly perform while walking around your organization. Pretend you are a customer, request and imagine yourself going through each step of your process. Don't ask people what happens; walk around, look at the data, find out for yourself.

Now that we have spent time on Eliminating Waste let's look at the next Lean Software Development principle, and that is Build Quality In.

Build quality/integrity in

Quality issues in your code can result in all kinds of waste. There's waste in testing the code more than once, waste logging defects, and waste in fixing them. As a result, lean principles aim to address this point. Agile methodologies such as Scrum and XP have practices that help you build quality into your development process. These practices are Pair Programming and Test-Driven Development.

Pair Programming helps to avoid quality issues in your code by using the minds of two developers at a time on each task. The task at hand then benefits from the combined experience of two developers at a time instead of one. The benefit of doing this is that it results in better overall productivity as the two developers see solutions that individually they may not have spotted. Another advantage of Pair Programming is the improved quality of the source code because one programmer can be thinking ahead of the other, catching issues before they occur.

Test Driven Development helps to avoid software quality problems by coding the tests before writing the actual implementation code. Good quality unit tests should stub out and isolate any dependencies in the code like accessing the file system, calling web API's, or accessing the database. By stubbing out these external dependencies, you can control what data gets returned to the code under test which lets you test multiple different scenarios.

Both pair programming and unit testing come from Extreme Programming, and both seek to prevent quality issues from occurring in the first place. The idea is to trap quality issues soon before they become an issue later. Building quality in doesn't just necessarily mean introducing better testing earlier in the development process. Building quality in is also about introducing monitoring into your project to allow you to see how your system is performing when it is deployed in production.

This could mean having good error logging, monitoring solutions, keeping an eye on your website and services. Infrastructure monitoring where you are looking at processor, memory and disk utilization. If you start running low on memory, you want to be alerted.

When you are performing real-time monitoring, you might want to look at that data over time so you can spot trends. Is your system getting gradually slower, do you have traffic spikes at certain times in the day or week? All this diagnostics information can then be fed back into your development team so that they can keep the system running efficiently and remaining to generate value for your customers.

Amplifying learning

The next lean principle we are going to look at is that of amplifying learning. Software development is a continuous learning process based on iterations when writing code. Software design is a problem-solving process involving the developers writing the code and what they have learned through the act of writing that code. Software value is measured in fitness for use and not in conformance with requirements.

Instead of writing lots of documentation or performing lots of detailed planning for a product, different ideas could be used to learn more about the customer's requirements. For example, based on conversations with the customer, you can build a series of wireframe mock-ups of any screens in the system which you present to the customer to comment on. This could happen over several revision cycles to narrow down how they expect the system to work.

During those short revision sessions, both customers and the development team will learn more about the requirements and the problems that are trying to be solved. This means the customers will better understand their own needs and the developers learn how to satisfy those needs better.

Here are some things to think about.

Feedback

The first is rapid feedback. You should introduce and increase feedback loops within the development process. For example, when you write some code, write unit tests and run them on each build. If a test fails because you broke something you will find out straight away instead of weeks down the line when a tester tries the software out. This helps you to keep you defect count as close to zero as you can get.

When looking at requirements, try making prototypes and showing them to your customers. This will give the customer the chance to have a look at what you are building and feedback into the development process much sooner. There is nothing worse than building something, and then your customer later down the line says this not what they intended.

Iterations

Short development iterations also help to amplify learning as they reduce the feedback and learning time from the initial design through to development, testing, and deployment. If you relate this to queueing theory, then you are delivering small batches regularly through an efficient development pipeline. This allows feedback to increase which give you more control over when you are delivering.

Decide as late as possible

The next lean principle we are going to look at is deciding as late as possible. The best decisions are made for a product when you have the most information available to help you. If you don't have to make a particular decision now, wait until later when you have more knowledge and information. But don't wait too long, a lack of a decision should not hold up other aspects of the project. Wait until the last sensible moment to make a decision that could be difficult to change later.

As an example, you may produce a specific type of calculation, a credit score for example, and there may be different choices in how you do this. Ideally, you want to defer this commitment until you have to make a choice. If for example, there are three ways of calculating this credit score, you might start work on all 3 and structure your code solution in a way where you can swap out the implementations easily. By trying all 3 of the solutions, you can collect data on the results and then make a better-informed choice for your customers. This is called set-based design where you simultaneously implement multiple solutions, eventually choosing the best one.

This could fit any scenario where you have to make decisions on your product; you could have an architectural decision to make, like do you use an enterprise service bus like NServiceBus or a message broker like RabbitMQ. You could experiment with both and see which one works best for you. By experimenting with two solution ideas, you build up valuable knowledge to make an informed decision.

Deliver as fast as possible

The next principle to look at is to deliver as fast as possible. In this day and age, it is the fastest to implement and deliver that survives and not the biggest. If you can get your product out into the market sooner, then you will be getting feedback sooner, and that will allow you to learn and improve. Delivering fast ensures that you can fulfil what a customer needs today instead of what they required yesterday. This lets them delay making critical decisions up front as they are getting versions of their software early to use and help inform any decisions that need to be made. Your customers will thank you for this rapid delivery as it gives them value sooner, but also provides them with confidence in a development team ability to deliver as opposed to more extensive big bang delivery schedules in a more traditional waterfall approach.

The just-in-time production ideology from the Toyota Production System could easily be applied to software development if it takes into account software developments specific requirements and environment. You can do this by allowing your development team to self-organize and be responsible for splitting and allocating the tasks between themselves for any given sprint or iteration.

When you start creating a product, the customer will need to provide input. This could be via user stores, and the development team then produce estimates for how long they think it will take to develop each story. This means the organization changes into a self-pulling system where each morning in a stand-up meeting, team members review what was done yesterday and then decide together what needs to be achieved today.

Software requirements are very volatile and can change over time. With the more traditional waterfall software development approach, you would have to wait until the end of the project to obtain feedback from your customers based on their actual use of the software. This means the Waterfall process is prone to failure because it does not allow got getting regular feedback from your customers.

To deliver fast means that you need to develop features in small batches or iterations that are given to the customer as soon as possible. This means that your customer can use these delivered features to provide feedback that can influence future requirements before too much time has been invested in their development. This continual refinement through customer feedback will ensure you deliver a better overall product.

Empowering the team

The next lean principle is that of empowering the team. There has been a traditional belief in most businesses about the decision-making in the organization where the managers tell the developers how to do their own job. When practicing Lean, the roles are turned where the managers listen to their developers instead of just issuing orders to them. This means the manager's purpose is to serve their developers, listen to their feedback and so anything possible to let the developers succeed on the product.

The lean approach favours the approach of finding good people and let them do their job, and not dictate to them how to do their job. This encourages progress, catches errors, and helps to remove impediments stopping the team from working.

A traditional and mistaken belief in a lot of companies is that their people are merely resources and numbers. Under lean, this attitude has to change. Your people, whether software developers, testers, or anyone else, are there to do much more than just complete a list of tasks. Your people will be your most significant source of input and feedback into the running of the company or team but for this to be productive people they need to be motivated and feel as though they have a higher purpose in the organization. Your development team should be allowed to speak to the end customer directly instead of going through an intermediary, and the team leaders and managers should be expected to support their teams and help out in any stressful situations. It is also the managers' responsibility to ensure that scepticism and negativity do not damage the teams' spirit as this can drastically affect productivity.

A large part of the motivation is finding meaning in your work and allowing a team to own their work. I once worked at a financial service company, and we wanted to find a way of getting customers who ordinarily would not pay back their debts to make payments. We had some ideas around allowing the customers to self-serve their debt payments and use positive reinforcement messages instead of the usual "pay us back, or you will incur penalties" messages. But we weren't entirely sure it would work.

Before investing a significant amount of effort into something that may not work out, you should try out a proof of concept first. A proof of concept will be a throwaway piece of code just to prove whether a theory will work or not. When a team writes a proof of concept, they don't even bother writing unit tests for them, as the code is never destined to be production code, but to learn from. You can think of this prototyping as a way to produce a minimum viable product.

We tried this in the team I was leading at the financial services company. For a self-service debt payment system, we wanted a self-service portal on the web to allow customers who are already in debt to make a payment online and therefore avoiding an awkward conversation with our debt collectors over the phone. The idea made a lot of sense, but before investing a significant amount of money in building the portal, we did a lean start-up style set of experiments to test the theory against a minimum viable product.

A couple of my developers put a basic set of pages together that hooked up to a payment processor. We had a system that could send out SMS messages from a CSV file, so we could limit the pool of customers who tried the system. This system sent an SMS message to a customer with a URL that contained an encrypted query string. This query string contains their account balance, and authentication details so we could do a basic security check on the customer. Once a customer has passed the security check they could make a payment via the payment processor. Then via a manual process, we could pull a list of the payments and apply them to our debt management system. The system wasn't perfect by any stretch, and it had some manual processes, but it only took a few weeks to get live, and we tested it against different target populations of customers.

From this, we learned that if you removed some of the barriers for a customer who is already in debt (missed their usual repayment dates) and allowed them a way to pay without having an awkward conversation, then they would be more likely to engage with us and pay. They just didn't want to talk to someone on the phone. We even had customers who were over three months' delinquent that come to the site and clear their balances because the barriers had been removed.

From this prototype and minimum viable product, we initiated a more extensive program of work to implement the system correctly. This experiment could have quickly gone the other way though. We could have built the experimental site, tried it with the same demographic of customers and no one would make a payment. It is better to try this via a series of experiments first than to pay for a much larger and expensive project only to have it make no impact at the end of the project.

When the team saw the results with people making a payment they were very motivated as they could see tangible results from the prototype where people were coming into the system and making payments.

The key message here was that the team was empowered to tackle this problem. We were given the remit of finding a way to get these already delinquent customers paying back their debts instead of us referring them to debt collection agencies. We had specific legal frameworks we had to operate in, and we worked with the business to ensure we were compliant, but the team owned the problem and developed the prototype, analysed the results and off the back of this learning a more extensive project was initiated to develop the real system.

Seeing the whole

Now let's look at the final of the Lean Principles, and that is seeing the whole. One of the big shifts in Lean thinking from a mass production mentality is discarding the belief that you need to optimize each step in a value stream. Instead, to increase the efficiency of the production process, look at optimizing the flow of value from the beginning of the production cycle to the end.

If you look back at the value stream example from earlier in the book; the funding approval stage took ten days. You may decide to try and optimize that first, but a bigger problem is that from the business wish list coming in, to the funding approval stage takes 30 days. Those 30 days are a waste, surely that would be a better thing to fix first?

Thinking back to the analogy of a production line, getting each machine to work as efficiently as possible does not work as well as maximizing the efficiency of the production flow in its entirety. Focus on the whole process – from the beginning (concept) to the end (consumption by the customer).

In the manufacturing space, the problem with optimizing each step is that it creates enormous inventories between the stages. In the software world, these "inventories" represent partially done work, for example, requirements completed, but not designed, coded, or tested.

Lean proved that one-piece flow (that is, focusing on building an item in its entirety) is a much more efficient process than concentrating on developing all of its parts faster. Inventories hide errors in the process. In the physical world, they may represent construction errors. In the software world, they may conceal misunderstandings with the customer (requirements), or poor design (design documents), or bugs (coded but not tested code), or integration errors (coded, tested, but not integrated code) or any number of other things. The more extensive the inventory, the more likely there will be undetected errors.

Applying Lean Software Development

In the previous chapter, we looked at the seven principles of Lean which were:

Eliminate waste: You should only spend time only on what adds real customer value.

Amplify learning: If you have tough problems, you increase feedback.

Decide as late as possible: Keeping your options open as long as practical, but no longer.

Deliver as fast as possible: Delivering value to customers as soon as they ask for it.

Empower the team: Letting the people who add value to your customers use their full potential.

Build integrity in: This is about not trying to tack on integrity and monitoring after the fact but building it in from the start.

Seeing the whole: You should beware of the temptation to optimize parts of the system at the expense of the whole.

Now let's revisit our fictional company and apply some of this thinking to their project.

There is no right answer when applying lean, and what we talk about in this chapter with Deltasoft is not a definitive answer. What this chapter should do is get you thinking about how you can apply some of these principles to your own projects and teams.

Let's start off by looking at our first principle, Eliminating Waste.

Eliminate Waste - The 7 Wastes

When we initially looked at Eliminating waste in the previous chapter, we first talked about seven types of waste in software development, these were.

- Defects

- Extra Features

- Handoffs

- Delays

- Partially Completed Work

- Task Switching

- Unneeded Processes

Let's go through this one by one and see how Deltasoft plans to deal with them. In the real world, it is tough to eliminate all of these, but being able to recognize these wastes and having an idea if how to deal with them is what is important here.

Defects

The vast majority of defects are easily avoidable if you have a little discipline. The developers Phil, Sarah, Peter, Hitesh, and Oliver, will try to mitigate errors with a high standard of unit, integration, and automated UI testing.

Their unit tests will cover small functional units of code and will not touch external resources like the database, file system or other external services. These will achieve this by proper use of interface-driven design and dependency injection so that when they develop their unit tests, they can inject mock objects of these external dependencies and fake the results that come back. This means they can do quite fine-grained testing of each piece of code they develop.

The integration tests are there to test more of the interactions between different code modules. Integrations tests are more likely to call external dependencies like the database or web services. Integration testing is much harder to do in an automated fashion, but the team has built a test environment that has all the system components deployed in and they inject clean test data each time they do a test cycle, so they can get predictable results from the tests.

The 3rd area of testing they are going to focus on is automated UI testing. The team's testers Douglas and Amanda are both experienced in Selenium, a web testing framework that lets you either do record and playback of test steps on the UI or by writing code to engineer UI tests. They aim to automate as much of their test cases as possible which leaves the remaining edge cases to manual testing.

Another area the development team aims to reduce defects is by keeping an eye on their code metrics. Code metrics available to the programmers, who use Microsoft Visual Studio, for example, are;

- **Cyclomatic complexity**, which is used to indicate the complexity of a program. It is a quantitative measure of the number of linearly independent paths through a program's source code.

- **Maintainability Index,** which calculates an index value between 0 and 100 that represents the relative ease of maintaining the code.

- **Depth of Inheritance,** which indicates the number of class definitions that extend to the root of the class hierarchy. The deeper the hierarchy the more difficult it might be to understand where particular methods and fields are defined or redefined.

- **Class Coupling**, which measures the coupling to unique classes through parameters, local variables, return types, method calls, generic or template instantiations, base classes, interface implementations, fields defined on external types, and attribute decoration. And finally

- **Lines of Code**, which indicates the approximate number of lines in the code.

These metrics give you an excellent visual indicator of the health of your code base. They won't tell you that the code is working as expected, that's what the unit tests are for, but they help give a good indication of the quality of the code itself.

The team will also be using code productivity tools like Resharper, or Code Rush to help enforce their coding standards. Code standard documents these days are a thing of the past. It is more common to use a tool like Resharper or Code Rush to analyze the code as you are typing, and it will come up with suggestions to improve the code by applying a set of rules. The team will decide which rules they want to enforce or not and it is the team's responsibility to ensure that any code warnings highlighted by the tools are fixed.

If on occasion the team does encounter a production defect, they have agreed with them that they will adopt a drop everything and fix mentality to try and ensure zero errors in production. The goal will be to fix, test and deploy a code fix as quickly as possible.

Extra Features

The next type of waste to look at is Extra Features. The team's workload will be governed by a backlog of work items that are initially curated by Sam the product owner and business analyst, Scott the scrum master and John, the development manager. Working with the business, they ensure that only the features that are required to deliver on the value streams are needed. This is reflected in the backlog as a series of prioritized work items. It is this list of work items that the development team uses to allocate their work.

The team has a philosophy of just writing enough code to satisfy a requirement and nothing more. For developers, it can be tempting to write lots of smart code and frameworks to anticipate future support needs on a project, but this extra code, as smart as it may be, is a waste. It is better just to write what is needed at the time. If over time when adding new features, they need to extend any of this code into a framework, it can be done later if it is required.

There is an acronym called YAGNI which means "You aren't gonna need it" is a principle of extreme programming that states a programmer should not add functionality until deemed necessary.

XP co-founder Ron Jeffries has written:

> "Always implement things when you actually need them, never when you just foresee that you need them."

Handoffs

Our next waste to take into consideration is that of Handoffs. In a waterfall project, you get handoffs at every stage of the project development lifecycle. The act of handing off documents is very wasteful as you lose some knowledge along the way as well as being time-consuming to get through all the handoffs. The team at Deltasoft try to avoid these handoffs by running as an Agile Scrum team. They were previously a waterfall team, but with their last project, they went more agile.

This means there will be no substantial documents that have to be written upfront and passed through various handoff stages. The team works with user stories which will be fleshed out by Sam, the product owner, several sprints before the developer are due to work on the code. This gives Sam time to sit with the business and work through the requirements. These user stories are then broken down into a series of backlog items that the team will use as the basis of their estimation and delivery.

The team will still produce document artefacts as part of the sprint, but they try to keep these in diagram form and put them on the wall. Scrum doesn't mean you write no documentation ever. You can still produce documents, but they have to add value and meaning to the team.

Delays

The next waste that we will mention is that of delays. Sam is the team's business analyst and product owner. He spends a lot of his time talking about the business and capturing their requirements for the product. These requirements end up as use cases that require fleshing out with enough detail for the developers to create backlog items.

As we just discussed, this happens a few sprints ahead of when the team needs the information. This is to ensure that there is no delay for the development team when they have to work on the features. They will have all the information they need to be able to start developing the features. If Sam didn't work ahead like this, then the team would have to spend a lot of time talking about the business when they are supposed to be writing the code, and this would cause delays.

Partially Completed Work

Our next waste to investigate is that of partially completed work. The team will aim to achieve all work by only writing the code that is required to satisfy that requirement, but there is always the possibility that priorities and requirements will shift which means that the team has to work on something else partway through the development of a feature.

Agile teaches us that embracing change is a good thing and it should be embraced, and it certainly should, but any code that has been partially written and not delivered into the hands of the customer is a waste. The code will linger around in the codebase and not be adequately maintained. It will be partially tested, and in extreme circumstances, a developer that doesn't realize that this is not a completed code may make it a dependency.

If this happens and the team is forced to work on something else which leave some features partially completed, the team will remove the code so that it is not in the main codebase and create a tag in the source control system, so they can retrieve a copy of it at a later date.

This ensures that no incomplete code is left in the production code base. The team can still get this code back at a later date and use it as long as they tag the code with something sensible to make it easier when searching for it. You can still get wasted costs from this partially completed work as time and money has already been spent on writing it, but that would have to be managed on a case by case basis.

Task Switching

The penultimate waste is that of task switching. When the team does its sprint planning, they will try to make sure that a developer only works in one area and that any tasks related to that area go to the same developer. This will allow the developer to focus on what they are doing without having to do a complete mental shift to another train of thought.

The team will try to minimise disruption to the sprint as best as they can, and Scott the Scrum Master will try to enforce this. As we previously mentioned, changes in requirements are to be expected and embraced, but this needs to be managed carefully by the Scrum Master so that the team is not always flip-flopping between tasks.

The team will always be more productive and therefore adding value if they can focus on a particular set of tasks. Switching between different tasks requires a sizeable mental shift which causes delays and is not efficient and therefore a waste.

Unneeded Processes

The final waste was Unneeded processes. This team at Deltasoft has come from a Waterfall background, so they are familiar with and have had to endure with excessive, unneeded procedures, and it is an area they are very keen not to go back to.

Previously, when they needed to deploy software they had to fill out a change request form on the intranet that included the reason for the deployment and a list of instructions on how to implement and roll back the software. For one of the teams last projects when working under a waterfall process, this deployment document was a 13-page word document. The change request required five people to sign off on the change, and this needed at least a four-day lead time to arrange before the change window starts.

Now the team has set up a continuous integration and delivery pipeline. When they check in code, this triggers a build that compiles the code, runs all the tests and packages up the deployment. This is then automatically deployed to a test environment. This candidate build can then be looked at by the testing team. If this build is passed by the testing team, who run a mixture of automated UI tests and manual exploratory tests that same build package is then deployed into the staging environment. Again, a series of automated tests are executed to smoke test the deployment in another environment. If all of these tests pass, then the candidate release package is allowed to be deployed into production.

Deltasoft has changed their deployment process so that if a candidate builds passes tests in all of these environments, then the build is authorized to go into production as it has passed through all these testing stage gates.

When the code is deployed into production, it is done using a zero-downtime deployment model; this means half of the load balanced infrastructure is deployed too and first leaving half of the servers untouched. If the deployment is ok in the first set of servers, then the code is implemented to the remaining servers, and they are put back into the load balancer.

If there is an issue with the deployment, the deployed servers are taken out of the load balancer and replaced with the original untouched servers. This means that there is minimal disruption in production. This means the first set of servers can be rolled back or rebuilt without effective service.

This means that it is possible for a build to go from check-in and into production in a few hours instead of having a lead time of nearly a week. Not every candidate build will flow into production. The team can choose which ones go out, but they can do this themselves with a minimal process in place that still provides an audit trail of how code flows into production.

In a sizeable regulated company, there will always be a need to process, but it can be straightforward for a process to become overbearing. In the example, we have just looked at Deltasoft have reduced the waste in their existing deployment process by eliminating the lead time for arranging deployments and also automating the actual deployment process, but they still have controls in place. The code has to pass through several environments, and all automated tests need to pass as well as some exploratory testing by the testers. This gives control to the process instead of code just idly being deployed into the test environments. This does emphasize disciple around their unit testing, integration testing, and automated user interface testing.

Eliminate Waste - Value Stream Mapping

In the previous chapter, we took a brief look at value stream mapping when talking about eliminating waste. The example we used was the value map of a business making a feature request through to a funding decision, implementation and then deployed to the company so it can make use of the feature.

This gave us the total cycle time of the idea from inception to deployment, and a sense of value-add time and non-value-added time. This lets us calculate how efficient the value stream is.

Now, let's take a look at some different examples that are relevant to the business domain at Deltasoft. Although Deltasoft is a functional company, these examples are relatively realistic to business domains that I have worked with before in financial services.

The examples start off with a customer applying for a new loan and end with the funds being dispersed into their bank accounts. For this example, we are only focusing on a happy path case where the customer is approved for the loan. As you can probably agree, there can be many different paths through a process like this, but I am using this particular example to illustrate the point of an inefficient process and a more efficient process.

First of all, the loan application process is very manual. The loan decision and identity checks being performed are all manual jobs that require human intervention. As you can imagine, the timings can be different for each customer, so these are based on average times from a sample of customers.

Let's take a look at this further.

New Loan : Manual Decision

Value vs Non Value	Results
Cycle Time	207 hours (8 days)
Value Add Time	3 hours
Non Value Add Time	204 hours
Efficiency %	3 / 207 = 0.9%

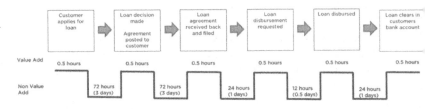

New loan value stream with manual decisioning

Here we have the customer making a loan application. This takes them about half an hour to do and then submit the loan details. The loan then goes into a queue waiting for someone to perform the credit checks. This can take up to 3 days. Once the agent starts working on that application, their checks usually take around half an hour. Then the loan agreement is printed out and sent to the customer where they have to sign the documents and send them back. This can take up to 3 days because of the time it takes to post letters.

Once the documents come back, they are opened and filed so the next part of the process can start. This filing takes up to half an hour. Then within the next 24 hours, the loan is finalized, and a payment disbursement is requested. When this is processed, the disbursement takes up to half an hour, and all the documents and records for the customer are set up including the payment schedule.

Then within the next 24 hours, the money appears in the customer's account. The total value-add time is 3 hours. This is the time where something is happening that will benefit the customer's request. The total non-value-added time is 204 hours due to the amount of waiting that is required either in manual processes or the postal system.

This makes the total cycle time, which is the value-add and non-value add time added together as 207 hours, or 8 days from loan application to funds appearing in the bank. If you divide the value-add time by the cycle time, this gives an efficiency score of 0.9%. It sounds awful when you put it like that, doesn't it?

Deltasoft realized that this process for banks was very inefficient, and their customer (banks and financial services companies) were losing competitive advantage over their competitors. When they designed their electronic loan platform, they optimised the new loan process to the following.

New Loan : Automatic Decision

Value vs Non Value	Results
Cycle Time	7.5 hours
Value Add Time	2.5 hours
Non Value Add Time	5 hours
Efficiency %	2 / 8 = 33%

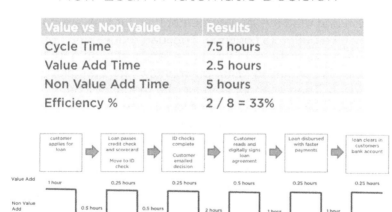

New loan with automatic decision

The loan application process for the customer this time can take a little longer, up to an hour. This is because the credit checks web service being used requires a reasonable amount of data points to make a valid decision. Once the customer hits submit, they are told they will receive a decision soon, so they don't have to sit there waiting.

The loan goes into a processing queue. At high load, it might be up to a max of half an hour before the credit check process starts. And this can take up to 25 minutes to complete the call to the credit reference agency, and this is also an asynchronous process. Once this has happened and the customer passes the credit check, the loan goes back into a processing queue for up to half an hour again, assuming high volume load.

The ID and verification checks for the customer can take again up to a max of minutes to process. If the customer passes, the customer is emailed with a link where they can re-join the loan process. This can take up to 2 hours as the customer may not be sitting at a machine or read their email for a few hours.

The customer then should read through all their details again and read the loan agreement, and if they are happy they hit a button to continue. The loan request then goes into a funds disbursement queue, and within an hour the money is sent using faster payments which can take up to 15 mins. Then in about an hour, the money will be available on the customer's account. The total Value add time in this example is 2.5 hours and the entire non-value add time which is process wait time under load is 5 hours.

This makes the total cycle time from customer application to funds being paid 7.5 hours, which is 33% efficient. This is a drastic improvement over the older manual process. These are simplified examples, but you can see the difference between the manual process and the newer automated process. Is the new method entirely efficient, no it is not? Is it better than before? Yes, it is.

This can still be improved further, and by mapping out this value stream, you can start to see where any bottlenecks are and with this holistic oversight of the entire value chain you can optimise the process as a whole instead of just focusing on small parts of the machine.

Let's now take a look at the next Lean Software Development applied to Deltasoft, which is Amplify Learning.

Amplify learning

As we have already covered, the Amplify Learning principle is about increasing a team's learning about the system they are building. Let's look at how Deltasoft is approaching this from 4 angles:

- Feedback

- Iterations

- Knowledge sharing

- And Code reviewing

Feedback

The team at Deltasoft want to get rapid feedback about the code that they are writing. To get this quick feedback, they are disciplined with test driven development and develop unit tests to a high coverage level. They strive for around 80% test coverage across their code base. This is isolated unit tests that run on each build, and they can't check code in unless the whole test suite is passing.

They also write integration tests that routinely run in a test environment, and the test results are displayed on a dashboard, so they can instantly see if there have been any failures.

Because they physically can't check in code until the tests are passing, this gives them the impetus to keep the tests high quality and the development manager John routinely reviews the unit tests to check the quality and to make sure people are not just disabling any tests.

Iterations

The team also work in short iterations to ensure that they can get functionality out to the end user quickly. This means the end users get small increments of functionality regularly instead of large pieces of functionality all at once.

Because they get these features out quickly, the end users can give feedback to the development team much quicker than if they have to wait a long time for new features. It is entirely possible that after the end user has played with some of this functionality that they may decide they want some changes to the requirements, and this is fine because it is better to incorporate this rapid feedback and course correction sooner than later.

This all makes the customer and end user much happier in the long run as they feel as that they are getting to collaborate more on the development of their system which is much harder to do if they have to wait longer to get their hands on new features.

Knowledge sharing

The team likes to share knowledge with each other and to make this easier they have set up a wiki where they share information. This includes things like documentation for setting up their development environment, solutions to common coding problems that team members have previously solved and as a repository for any documents and diagrams for their project work.

The team is also encouraged to use online knowledge sharing sites like Stack Overflow and Stack Exchange as they are great sites for both getting help and also contributing answers back into the community and the team is encouraged to do this, provided of course they don't divulge any company proprietary information.

Code reviewing

Finally, for amplifying, learning the Deltasoft team perform lots of code reviews. They sometimes do pair programming, but not all the time. When they do not pair programming, they have a rule where the will perform code reviews with another developer when checking in large blocks of code. They don't necessarily do this for every check-in if it is a small and low impact change, but they will do it for more extensive check-ins.

The team also runs regular lunchtime code reviews sessions. They do this on a Wednesday lunchtime. The developers all get together, and they can bring their lunch, and they go through a subsection of the code on the projector. The idea of this is to get people familiar with different parts of the code base that they may not use every day. This helps make all the developers on the team to be multi-functional as anyone should be able to work on any part of the system.

Build integrity in

The next lean principle to apply to the team at Deltasoft is that of "building integrity in" The team will take some measures for building integrity into their system. First, from a code level, they will use extensive instrumentation and logging using tools like Raygun.NET or Stackify to record logs and errors in a central place. This will allow them to not only observe problems as they occur but also try to do some pre-emptive detection of a problem that may arise in the future by looking at trends in errors that occur. This coupled with a high level of unit, and integration testing gives them a lot of oversight on the quality of their code, and it's running in production.

The team will also keep an eye on the built in the code quality metrics available in visual studio and use these as the basis of code reviews. This will allow the team to look at maintainability indexes and Cyclomatic complexity for classes and methods being reviewed. These metrics give an instant visual feedback identifier for the code being written and discussed. For examples, if the Cyclomatic complexity of a method goes over 8, this might indicate that the method is getting too large and complex and therefore making it harder to read and maintain which means they should separate this code out into smaller, well-defined methods.

Another area where the team will try to maintain high integrity and quality of their product is via the enforcement of coding standards. It is traditional that a team may have a coding standards document, but it is tough to follow one of these documents rigidly and even harder to write a good one, so the team at Deltasoft doesn't seem intent to use a document like this at all.

Instead, they will use tools to help enforce adherence to coding standards. These tools cover two areas, as you type coding standards and static code analysis.

For the "as you type" coding standards they will use coding productivity tools like Resharper, CodeRush, JustCode or Visual Assist which warn the developer of any violations as they are typing. This is generally by a little-coloured bar at the side of the coding window. These tools even offer tips to a developer on how to fix the issues. The great thing about these tools is that they are easy to use, and you can make sure each developer is working on the same set of rules.

The team also intends to use static code analysis. Microsoft Visual Studio allows you to quickly apply static code analysis rules to a project that are executed each time you run a build. These will give you either warnings or errors, which you can configure. These rules can look at naming conventions, how you allocate and dispose of an object and many other rules.

I have used static code analysis rules many times in companies that I have worked for. I have found that if you are starting fresh, then set the rules to be quite strict from the start. If you are working on an older legacy project, then I suggest starting off with a limited rule set and then increase the number of rules over time. Otherwise, you will overwhelm the team as all the builds will start failing.

The final area to look at here with regards to integrity is having a monitoring and alerting solution that runs on your infrastructure and monitors server's memory allocations, disk IO, network IO, etc. You can also have these monitoring tools keeping an eye on your services, web servers, and sites, etc. and set to alert if anything goes down. A lot of these tools will also look at data over time to calculate trends, so you can be given early warning to any problems, like memory leaks, or running out of disk space.

Decide as late as possible

The next principle to apply to Deltasoft is decide as late as possible. To demonstrate this principle, we have an example where Sam the business analyst and product owner has been talking with the business about KPI reporting which stands for key performance indicators. This is where the company can have a dashboard view that shows critical metrics from the business.

While the business knows what KPI metrics they want, they haven't decided how they want them to be calculated. This isn't a problem for the development team though as they can structure their code in a way where this decision on the calculations can be deferred. The team does this by structuring their KPI calculation code using the strategy design pattern.

This is where you can have a default implementation for a calculation and then using dependency injection, substitute a different implementation of the calculation later on. The benefit of this is that the team can lay all the groundwork for the dashboard, and the calculation logic while the business is deciding how they want to perform the actual calculations. Once the company determines how they want this done, the developers will just write new strategy substitutions to swap out the default implementations.

Deliver as fast as possible

The next principle is that of delivering as fast as possible. The team aims to release features into production regularly. Ideally, they will release code every sprint onto the production servers. This means that the team will be working on several features at the same time, effectively splitting the team into small sub-teams. One design goal of the group is that every feature being worked on has to have an on/off switch that allows them to disable features on release. This means that they can quickly release code regularly and anything that is not ready to be used in production can be disabled so the end users can't access it.

This fast delivery is supported by the judicious amount of unit, integration, and UI automation testing. As the release frequency increases, the reliance on automated becomes even more critical. This is all backed up by a continuous integration and delivery that automates all aspects of test execution, build packaging and deployment to target servers. We will be talking about continuous integration and delivery in a later chapter.

Empower the team

The penultimate principle to look at is that of empowering the team, and this is a fundamental principle to follow for the success of a team. John is the development manager and he believes that the team should be empowered and self-directing. This means John's role goes more from that of a typical top-down authoritative leader who tells the team what to do all the time to that of a servant leader where the team picks their tasks, and John helps to remove any problems that get in their way and sets their direction.

When the team works on a sprint, they don't get their work items allocated to them by John or Sam the business analyst. Instead, John and Sam ensure that before the start of each sprint, the team's unallocated backlog has been prepared and sorted into the correct priority order. Then when the team has a planning session, they can take the tasks they want to work on. They need to keep an eye on the order of priority for work as this is dictated by what needs to be delivered to the customer, but the team has the freedom to decide what they work on.

The team is also responsible for deciding what technology they use and how their deployment process operates. John, the development manager, does not dictate this. The team chooses their technology choices together, and this gives the team a good sense of empowerment. By allowing this empowerment, the team feels more motivated, and they get more meaning for their work. This is important for keeping a team engaged in what they are doing, especially during the tough and more stressful times as it helps impose a good sense of team camaraderie.

Seeing the whole

The final lean principle to cover is that of seeing the whole. This is a hard principle to discuss upfront for Deltasoft, but what this principle is talking about is not just optimizing individual parts of the value stream and look at the whole process as a whole.

New Loan : Manual Decision

Value vs Non Value	Results
Cycle Time	207 hours (8 days)
Value Add Time	3 hours
Non Value Add Time	204 hours
Efficiency %	3 / 207 = 0.9%

New loan manual decision

If you look back to our loans application value stream example from earlier in the book. Looking at the manual application process, you might be tempted to optimise just individual parts of that value stream like the credit checking or the identity verification process, but what was wrong was the total cycle time from customer application to the money being deposited into the customer's bank account. By looking at the process as a whole, the cycle time could be reduced significantly to where a loan could be applied for and funded within 8 hours.

New Loan : Automatic Decision

Value vs Non Value	Results
Cycle Time	7.5 hours
Value Add Time	2.5 hours
Non Value Add Time	5 hours
Efficiency %	2 / 8 = 33%

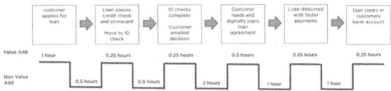

New loan automatic decision

Sam, our business analyst and the rest of the team will be looking at these holistic value streams as a whole to work with the business to try and optimize the entire process for the better instead of just tuning small parts of the system.

The same goes for optimizing the code that makes up the system. If you have bottlenecks in any area of the code, it is best to look at the system from a higher level instead of just performing micro-optimizations. These micro-optimizations might get you small marginal gains, but these may be at the expense of optimizing the whole system.

Agile vs Lean

Agile Benefits

Agile software development is an entirely different approach to software development compared to the more traditional Waterfall development model. Let's take a look at some of the benefits of using the Agile approach. If you want a more in-depth look at Agile Software Development, including Scrum and Extreme Programming, then I recommend my other book,

Customer satisfaction by rapid, continuous delivery of useful software

You want to keep your customers satisfied by continually delivering lots of value with software that works. The key term here is, continuously delivering, as opposed to the more traditional waterfall methodologies where you would provide a more significant big bang at the end of the project.

By continually delivering, you are also getting a return on your investment much sooner as opposed to just incurring project costs with no return on investment until the end of the project if any at all.

Agile is focused very heavily around people and the interactions between people rather than the processes and tools

This is a core value of the Agile Manifesto. It is important because it is the input from your team and customers that will ultimately make your project a success, as opposed to what software tools you use. Continual collaboration throughout the entire development cycle of your project enables everyone involved to build a good working relationship based on trust. This trust-based working relationship is crucial when building software incrementally.

Continuous attention to high quality code and design.

Agile working is helped by working in very short iterations and only building the minimum necessary to satisfy the requirements and stories defined for that iteration. This helps your system to seem simple which makes it easier to develop and test reliable systems.

Software developers tend to favour using the latest techniques and tools for making their software solutions clean and tested to help minimise rework in the future. This rework can be very wasteful if it is not helping the end customer achieve their goals sooner.

One of these techniques is refactoring. Refactoring is the gradual process of improving the structural design of existing code without changing its behaviour. To make changes to the structure of the code refactoring, you will need to use a quick succession of small, well-defined steps that can be verified as safe or functionally equivalent. Refactoring is most often done in conjunction with test-driven development where unit tests and simple design make it easier to refactor safely.

Simple design

By keeping your software design simple, and not repeating code, it helps you keep your system maintainable over time. If you design your code to be modular and interface-driven, then you can reduce coupling between objects, which leads to a more robust system.

Test-driven development

Test-driven development or TDD as it is commonly referred to is a way of evolving the design of your source code by writing a unit test, which documents what you intend that code to do. By making those tests pass, and continually refactoring to keep the design as simple as possible. TDD can be applied at multiple levels, for example, unit tests and integration tests. Test-driven development follows a rigorous cycle. You start off by writing a test that fails. Then you implement enough code that will cause that test to pass. Next, you search for duplication in the system and remove it. This is often called Red-Green-Refactor and has become almost a mantra for many test-driven design practitioners.

Embracing changes in requirements

When developing software for your customers, they reserve the right to change their minds with the requirements. Under Agile, this is perfectly fine and to be embraced. They may change their mind because what you have developed and delivered so far has given them different ideas about how to make their product better. They could also change their minds because the companies' priorities have changed.

The critical thing here is that you should embrace it. Yes, some code may get thrown away and some time is lost, but if you are working in small iterations, the amount of work lost can be minimal. Change can be terrifying at first for clients and partners, but when both sides are prepared to leap, it can be mutually rewarding. One of the key ideas with Agile is to be open to change, not just to move in traditional ways of organizing projects, but to adapt your use of Agile itself.

Early return on investments.

A major benefit of Agile software development is that you can release working software sooner to your customers by only building what is required at the right time in. This allows your customers to realize an early return on their investment by getting working software sooner. Of course, it will not have all the features they require up front, but they can start using it, feeding back, and making money with it.

This is especially important as software development teams are expensive to run, so if you can make money back earlier to help cover the costs, then this is a win-win situation. This is in stark contrast to the more traditional waterfall development methodology where all requirements are defined up front, which means changes midway through a product development have a high-cost impact to the team, and you only deliver as a big bang at the end of the development cycle, if at all.

Feedback from your customers.

With Agile, having the ability to release early allows you to solicit feedback from your end customer sooner. These customers could be public consumers or internal business customers; it doesn't matter as long as you get working software in their hands early for them to use.

Once you start getting feedback from real customers, you can start incorporating changes and new ideas from the feedback into the product. It is much more cost effective to make changes early on in a product's development cycle than it is to wait until the end after a large release has been made. It's not just customer feedback that helps you build the right product. By testing your product early in the marketplace, you can gauge customer uptake and see how popular the product will be, and continually deliver better quality.

Everything we have discussed so far has business benefits or culminates in the fact that you should be delivering a better-quality product with every release. By releasing earlier and soliciting feedback, you can learn from the product performance earlier, and use this information to create something better. Product and system development are all about continuous learning and improvement, which is much easier to do when you're delivering a project by being agile. It doesn't matter whether you're using Extreme Programming, Scrum, or any of the other project management frameworks. If you adhere to the core values in the Agile Manifesto and routinely deliver high-value functionality early to your customers, monitor their usage, and listen to their feedback, you can apply this learning to the ongoing development and increase quality as you go along.

Let's now take a look at the benefits of Lean software development.

Lean Benefits

The elimination of waste leads to the overall efficiency of the development process

This, in turn, speeds up the process of software development which reduces project time and cost. This is very important in today's environment. Anything which allows companies to deliver more projects in the same timeframe is going to be very beneficial to that company.

Delivering the product early is a definite advantage

It means your development team can provide more functionality in a shorter period, hence enabling more projects to be delivered. This will only please both your finance department, but also the end customers.

Empowerment of the development team helps in developing the decision-making ability of the team

By empowering a development team to make their own decisions, you will naturally create a more motivated team. Knowledge workers like software developers hate being micro-managed. Nothing is more frustrating than having decisions forced upon you. By empowering the team to make decisions, you will end up with a much better product at the end of it.

Now that we have looked at some of the benefits of Agile and Lean lets now look at what we should use?

Agile vs Lean

With everything that we have looked at so far, what's different about Lean software development and Agile software development? When you look from the outside in, there is not much difference.

Both of these methodologies are about improving the quality of the software for the end customer and improving the productivity of the development process. They also encourage and embrace changes in requirements and process, but most importantly they are both about delivering value, quickly, to the end user and customer.

Agile methodologies like Scrum primarily concern themselves with the practice of developing software and any activities that surround the developing of the software. Lean on the flip side can be applied to any scope from the development of the software itself so the entire business domain where the software development is just one small bit.

The main focus of an Agile software development is to focus on customer collaboration and the quick delivery of software. Lean software development also sees that as necessary, but its main focus is on the elimination of waste as we have discussed at length previously. An important tool for eliminating waste is value stream mapping which is a diagram that maps out all activities that take place in a business process from start to finish where you identify processes that add value and don't add value to the customer.

So, to answer the question of Agile or Lean? The answer makes the perfect combination together. Agile has some formal methodologies like Scrum and Extreme Programming, whereas Lean has no formal methodologies. Lean, instead, is a toolkit of recommended practices from which to choose.

Scrum is a common methodology to use when trying to apply lean thinking as it is relatively lightweight and early to learn and adapt.

A good way of thinking is as follows.

Scrum / Agile is a value driver software development framework.

Leans helps you to optimise its process.

You cannot DO lean. You USE lean to improve your process.

Software Practices to Support Lean

In this chapter, we will look at some standard technical practices you should use to help you be leaner in how you develop software. These are fairly standard practices in the industry these days, but it is worth calling them out as they help you to reduce waste with defects and to reduce feedback time from checking in code to getting a release out. These are not just applicable to Lean but are also standard practices for adopting agile methodologies like Scrum and Extreme Programming.

We will cover the following practices

- Source Control Repositories

- Continuous Integration and Deployment

- Automated Testing and TDD

We have mentioned these things throughout the book, but this chapter will bring them all together as if you get all of these right, you put yourself in a good position for implementing both Agile and Lean.

Let's dive in and look at Source Control Management.

Source Control Management

These days running a development team without any source control should be a thing of the past. I would even say it is one of the bare minimum pieces of development infrastructure that a team requires to operate safely and efficiently.

Source control is used primarily to retain the latest working set of files for your project and any previous revisions of each file. This means that you can safely go back to previous working sets of your solution should you need to.

Another huge benefit of source control systems is the ability to merge conflicts with other developers. If you have lots of developers working on the source code at once, it is inevitable that there will be times where their changes conflict. One way to resolve this is to say that if there is any conflict, then one of the developers must lose their changes and other developers are accepted, but this is not acceptable. What you need instead is a way for the source control system to detect these conflicts and allow the developers to merge their changes into the source repository. This makes it much easier for a team to develop code together knowing that they have a source control system watching their back.

There are 2 types of source control system that you will encounter. Those are Centralized and Distributed Source Control Systems.

Let's take a look at them both.

Centralized Source Control

An excellent way to visualize a centralized source control system is to imagine it as a hub and spokes, as you can see in the following diagram. The hub in the middle represents your server containing your source control system. This is where the central repository is held. Each spoke on the diagram represents a user accessing the source control system. When these users want to work on the code, they each take a copy of the code onto their local machines.

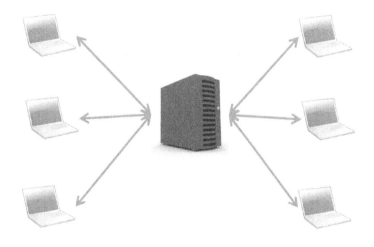

Centralized source control

There are many types of centralized source control system from Microsoft own offerings like the old SourceSafe to the newer and more modern Team Foundation Server to the open source varieties like Subversion, and CVS. There are of course many different vendors you can choose from in this category.

Once the user has a copy of the source code on their local machine, they can work on those files. To work on a file, they must "Checkout" that file which lets the central system know they are working on the file. Any files they work on like this go into a change set, so they can all be checked in together. To check files in and out of the source control system, the user has to be connected to that source control system on the network or over the internet. If they are not connected, then they lose the ability to check files in and out which makes working on your project very difficult and this is the main downside of using a central repository like this.

Another essential concept in centralized source control systems is that of branching. Branching, in source control systems, is the duplication of an object, like a source code file or any other asset, so that modifications can happen in parallel along both branches.

Branches are also known as code lines. The starting branch is often called the parent branch, mainline or trunk. Child branches are branches that have a parent. Branching also means you can later merge changes back onto the parent branch from a child branch.

Branching in source control

By using branches, you enable the team and parts of the product to be developed in parallel. By creating branches, the development team and isolate and work on changes separately without causing each other problems. Once they are done with their changes, they should merge them back together to form one complete working system.

Merging changes back into the main line

There are many patterns you can adopt when it comes to branching, and these are out of scope for this book, but the important message here is that branching is a fundamental feature to enable teams to co-work on a codebase at the same time.

Now that we have taken a look at centralized source control systems, lets now take a look at their counterpart, Distributed source control systems.

Distributed Source Control

Distributed source control systems instead take on a peer-to-peer approach to version control instead of the hub and spoke method of centralized systems. Instead of having a central repository on which the development team synchronizes each person's working copy of the codebase, they instead have a complete repository and version control system in its own right on their machines. Distributed source control systems synchronize repositories by exchanging patches, or sets of changes, from person to person. This is a fundamental difference to centralized source control systems.

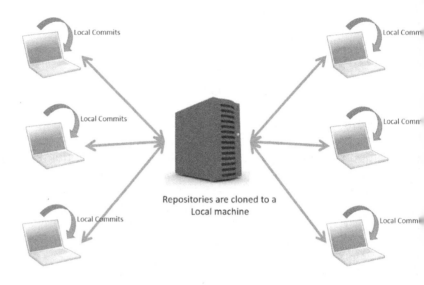

Distributed source control

There is no canonical or reference copy of the codebase that exists by default, only the working copies that each person has. Common source control features such as code committing, showing file history, and undoing changes are fast as there is no need to communicate back to a central server all the time. The complete code base is on the user's machine, and they make all their changes and commits to that local repository.

Communication back to a central repository is only required when sharing changes among other people at such a time that the code needs to be integrated back with other people's work. Each working copy functions as a remote backup of the codebase and its change-history, protecting against data loss. This means if you have a team of ten developers, then you effectively have 10 complete copies of the source tree and all its revision history.

Because of this distributed nature, it means that a developer can work disconnected from the network and internet as they are just operating against a local repository.

Again, there are many different types of distributed version control systems such as Git, Mercurial. These are both open source, free solutions. To make working with these systems easier, there are also some paid-for hosted solutions that make working with Git and Mercurial easier as they offer full workflow management tools as well as just source control. Two popular types of an online tool like this are Github and BitBucket.

When a team uses a distributed source control system like Git, there are some key terms that you will come across that you will need to recognize. These are Clone, Fork, Commit, Pull Request and Push. Let's take a quick look at each one.

Clone

A clone is a complete copy of a source code repository that sits on your computer instead of on a central server. Once you have cloned the codebase onto your machine, you can use your preferred code editor to work on that local copy. The distributed source control system will keep track of the changes you make on your local copy without having to connect back to the server.

Your machine is, however, connected to the remote version so that your changes can be synchronized between the two. You push your local code changes back up to the remote to keep them synchronized when you're online.

Fork

A fork is a copy of someone other user's repository that you make that lives on your source control account. This fork allows you to make changes to a project without affecting the original project. It is an entirely separate copy of that project that you will not merge changes back into. You can, of course, keep your fork up to date with changes from the original repository by merging their changes back into your branch.

Commit

A commit is when you save your changes back into your local copy of the repository. Every time you make this commit, you get a unique reference for that commit, so you can track the changes over time. When you commit changed files back into the repository, you usually provide a short commit message so that you document the intended purpose of that change.

Pull Request

When you have been committing files into your local repository, and you then want to send them back to the central repository, you create what is known as a pull request. The owner of the central repository can either accept or reject the pull request. The pull request lets you inform others about the changes you have pushed so they can merge them into the central code base. This is a good way of managing the flow of changes back into a more substantial project so that control can be maintained.

Push

Finally, we have the pushing of changes. Pushing refers to sending your committed changes to a remote repository such as GitHub.com. For instance, if you change something locally, you would then want to push these changes so that others may access them.

Now that we have taken a quick, high-level, look at Source Control Systems. Let's take this a further step in our quest to look at software practices to support lean. Let's take a look at Continuous Integration and Deployment.

Continuous Integration and Delivery

Continuous Integration integrates lots of code changes that have been submitted to your source control system together and performs a remote build which executes tests and packages a deployment.

The way this works is that a build is triggered every-time developers check in a change to source control. If the build fails, either by failing to compile, or tests failing then the code check-in is rejected, and the code is not stored in the repository until the developer fixes the problem. This is an excellent way of helping to ensure that the state of the code in your repository is always healthy that it builds and has a passing test suite.

There are some prerequisites to setting up a continuous integration system. First, you need to have a modern source code management system as we have already discussed in this chapter.

Next, you have to make sure you are using a unit testing framework that will allow you to execute automated tests. We will cover unit testing in more detail in the next clip, but at a high level, you want to be using a testing framework like NUnit, or MSTest in the Microsoft world or an equivalent in your chosen software development environment.

The next thing to consider when talking about Continuous Integration is that of having automated builds and a build server to carry out those builds. The idea is that a build is automatically triggered once a developer checks in their code; ideally, this would be on a server that is not the source control repository. This build would compile the code, run any unit tests, run any static code analysis and then package up the release. The good thing about using a separate server is that if you need to you can scale out to multiple servers if the load on the build server gets too much.

Some source control systems like Team Foundation Server already contain features for automating builds, but you can get 3rd party products like Team City from JetBrains or the open source Jenkins Continuous Integration system.

Once you have a build system in place, you then want the ability to deploy your compiled and test application to a test environment or production. A good deployment solution like Octopus Deploy, will let you build and package up a candidate build which is then deployed to a selected environment. A significant benefit of tools like Octopus deploy is that you can configure them only to let you deploy to environments in a specific, like dev, test, UAT, staging and then production.

This is important as it ensures you are promoting a release candidate build through to the correct environment. This release candidate is not rebuilt when it is deployed to each environment. It is built initially and deployed to say a development testing environment and once it has been tested (and passed) in that environment that the same build can be promoted to the next environment in the chain.

Developers and the CI Process

An efficient Continuous Integration process requires more than a collection of tools and scripts. It requires acceptance and agreement by the development team members to adopt them. This adoption should very much be a team decision. Continuous Integration works by integrating small pieces of functionality at regular intervals. Developers must adhere to a few rules to make the CI process efficient.

Frequent check-ins

Developers should check code into the source control repository at least once a day, preferably several times a day. The longer modified code remains checked out, the more likely it is to get out of sync with the rest of the project, leading to problems integrating the code when it is finally checked in.

Only check in functional code

Although code should be checked in often, it should not be checked in if it is not yet functional, doesn't compile, or fails unit tests. Developers must build the updated project locally and run the applicable unit tests before checking code into the repository. If you are using a gated check-in process where the build process has to run and pass before committing the code, then this rule is automatically enforced.

The highest priority task is fixing build failures

When a failure is detected in the build, fixing the failure becomes the highest priority. Allowing a build failure to persist adds the risk of integration problems to ongoing development, so developers need to focus on fixing the problem before moving forward.

Continuous Delivery is a topic that can be very broad and there are many patterns to setting it up. The book in the following image is called Continuous Delivery by Jez Humble and David Farley is considered the technical bible when it comes to continuous delivery. If you are interested in implementing continuous delivery, then I recommend buying their book.

Continuous Delivery by Jez Humble and David Farley

The book, in a lot of details, documents eight key principles of continuous delivery. I want to highlight them here for you.

Repeatable reliable process: Here you use the same release process in all environments. If a feature or enhancement has to work through one process on its way into the integration environment, and another process into QA, issues find a way of popping up.

Automate everything: You should automate everything you can with your project, builds, testing, releases, configuration, etc. Having manual processes are not easy to repeat and are more prone to errors. Once a process has been automated, it takes less effort to run it and monitor its overall progress.

Version control everything: Code, configuration, scripts, databases, documentation. Everything! Having one source of truth, and a reliable one gives you a stable foundation to build your processes upon.

Bring the pain forward: Here you are encouraging your team to deal with the hard stuff first. Time-consuming or error-prone tasks should be dealt with as soon as you can. Once you get the painful issues out of the way, the rest will most likely be more straightforward to perfect.

Build in quality: This is about creating short feedback loops that allow you to react to bugs as soon as they are created. An example of a feedback look might be a series of unit tests that fail on a build, indicating that a code change has broken some functionality. It is better to detect the failure here than it is to let the change go into production and be found later on when it is already affecting the customer.

Done means released: A feature is done only when it is in production. Having a clear definition of "done" right from the start will help everyone communicate better and realize the value in each feature.

Everyone is responsible: "It works on my computer" was never a valid excuse. Responsibility should extend all the way to production. Cultural change can be the hardest to implement. However, having management support and an enthusiastic champion will undoubtedly help.

Continuous improvement: This principle is especially crucial for automation. If "practice makes perfect" than automation is the next level – perfect, repeatable, reliable and efficient – perfecting your automation process is a key ingredient to bringing substantial return on investment to continuous delivery.

Now that we have looked at source control systems and continuous integration and deployment processes, let's take another look at automated testing and test-driven development. We have already alluded to the benefits of automated testing when discussing building integrity in as one of the lean software development processes, but I want automated testing out specifically while we are talking about software development best practices to support lean.

Automated Testing and TDD

Automated testing helps us build higher quality software as it reduces the feedback loop from detecting an error to fixing it. We have already covered how important this is to run a lean project as it enables the developer to detect and fix an issue while the code is still fresh in their mind. There are many different types of automated testing that you can perform. Let's summarize them now.

Unit Testing

Unit testing involves isolating small pieces of testable code in an application and writing tests that exercise that code to assert whether it is doing what it should be doing. Each unit test is testing code separately before the code under test is integration test altogether. It has been proven time and time again that writing effective unit tests at the time you are developing your code helps you reduce the number of defects that are found later.

With unit testing, it is common to stub out dependencies in your code so that you are only testing one thing. For example, if the code you are testing writes data back out to a database, then you would stub out the code that writes to the database and replaces it with a stub that doesn't access the database. This makes repeatable writing tests much more manageable.

Writing unit tests can be seen as a costly exercise by managers and project managers alike, and while it is true that they have an upfront cost, you will save money in the long run as you will not be chasing obscure defects.

Integration Testing

Integration testing is a natural extension of unit testing. In its purest form, two units that have already been unit tested are then tested together as a complete component. In the previous example, we talked about stubbing out a database for the unit test. In an integration test, we would test that code without the stub and want to verify that the data is written to the database.

Behaviour Driven Design Testing

Behaviour Driven Development (BDD) is a software development methodology where an application is designed by describing how its behaviour should appear to an outside observer.

A software development project would start with BDD by having the end customers or stakeholders offer examples of the behaviour that they expect to see from the system. The software development effort is then focused on delivering these desired behaviours.

By using these real-life examples from the customers, they are turned into acceptance criteria with a series of validation tests that the software development team can automate. The results of these automated tests provide confidence to stakeholders that their desired objectives for the software are going to be achieved.

Automated UI Testing

Automated UI testing is where you test your application from the outside in. This means you have a series of tests that use the user interface of your application as a real user would. The testing framework for UI testing usually allows you to work in 2 modes. The first is where you record the tests in a test recorder by actually using the software and recording your mouse clicks and keyboard keys being pressed. You can then play these tests back repeatedly. This type of testing is an excellent way of getting into automated UI testing as it doesn't require much intervention from the software development team. Your existing testing team can start recording the tests and use them in the future.

The only complication here is that if a tester records a test for a particular set of data, if that data is persisted in a database, then the next time you run that test it might be invalid. In this situation, it is normal that you do some environment reset to restore your data back to a known point. This can be done either by a database restore or starting with a blank database and then seeding enough data to make the application functional. Another technique in a system that uses user accounts is to have the automated tests create new user accounts each time and apply the tests to those accounts. This can easily be done by generating random email addresses or usernames.

The next level of automated UI testing is to use an API that lets you simulate button clicks from code. This is preferable to the record and playback as the code for these tests can then be checked in along with your normal source code, and you can get these automation tests to execute as a step of your build process when deploying to an environment.

Common tools for automated UI testing are Selenium and Watin for web application testing and tools like Coded UI for testing thick client application written in WPF or Winforms. That's a very Microsoft .NET approach, but all development environments that let you produce UI applications will have their testing frameworks. While they may be different in execution, fundamentally they all follow similar principles.

Performance Testing

Performance testing is about determining the speed or overall performance benchmark of an application of the system. This could involve measurements such as millions of instructions per section, millisecond timings and other timings of any system components.

Performance testing is used to verify that a system meets the performance specifications defined by its designers. The process can compare two or more applications regarding parameters like data transfer rate, overall speed, bandwidth or throughput. There are three main areas of performance testing. Load Testing, Stress Testing, and Soak Testing.

Load testing is the most common form of performance testing. This type of testing is conducted to understand how the system behaves under a specified amount of load.

This could be some concurrent users performing transactions at the same time, such as an online store. This type of testing will give response times to the transactions being performed so that the behaviour can be monitored over time.

Stress testing is normally used to see what happens to a system when it is pushed to its upper limits of capacity. This is to see how the system responds in times of extreme load. I used to work for a large retail company in the UK and stress testing of the main website used to be carried out to see how the site would respond on Black Friday and Cyber Monday.

The final type of performance testing is soak testing. It is also commonly referred to as endurance testing. This type of testing is performed to see if the system can sustain a continuous expected load over time. During these tests, you would monitor memory utilization for memory leaks, network latency, disk space usage, or any other system resource that can be impacted by the running of your system. Another thing to look out for with a soak test is whether your system will degrade in performance over time. Does a transaction on the system after 10 hours of running take longer to perform than a transaction performed in the first hour?

Excuses for not testing

Writing automated tests of any kind is a massive benefit, but they do come with an upfront development cost. I have worked in many companies before where when times get tough; testing is the first thing to get reduced. I am not saying that this is the correct behaviour, it's not, but this is a definite problem in a lot of companies.

What I have found that a lot of managers fail to see is that although there is an upfront cost to writing tests, they save you a lot of money further down the line, but the difficulty you will face when under pressure is convincing managers and project managers that this upfront cost is worth it.

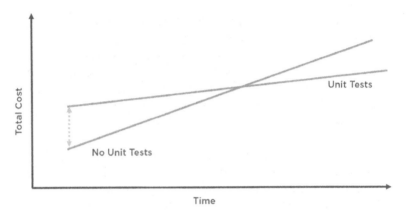

Cost of unit testing vs not unit testing

The chart in the preceding diagram sums this up perfectly. Look at the scenario where we have no tests. As time progresses, the total cost of the project increases as issues not detected upfront come back to bite you to have a higher cost to fix.

Now, look at the 2nd line. In the beginning, the cost is higher, but the line is flatter as over time the cost only marginally increases as you catch most problems earlier. The line does increase in cost, it is very hard to catch every scenario, but the key point is that the rise in cost is a lot less.

Kanban

In this chapter, we will take a look at another software development methodology that goes hand in hand with Lean Software Development, and this is Kanban. Kanban is a great way of organizing a lean software project, but it is different to Scrum in how it operates.

In this chapter, we will cover the background to Kanban and look at subjects such as Minimizing Cycle Time, Work in Progress limits and we will also take a look at Scrum vs. Kanban.

Kanban Background

As we looked at in our chapter on Lean Manufacturing, the techniques were initially discussed in the 1940's by Toyota when they studied supermarkets and their ideas of shelf stocking and how they could apply to the factory floor. With the supermarket example, customers would retrieve what they wanted at the required time. The supermarket stocks only what it expects to sell at any particular time and the customers only take what they need as they are confident that there will be a future supply.

The Kanban process that we are going to discuss in this chapter, regarding manufacturing, aligns inventory levels with actual consumption. Kanban uses a rate of demand to control a rate of production and passes demand from the end customer up through the entire chain of customer processes. This is what Toyota, in 1953, applied in their main plant machine shop.

When we relate this to software development, Kanban is a technique for managing the knowledge work of a team with an emphasis on just-in-time delivery. All this while not overloading the team members. The Kanban process gives all the participants, a software development team in this instance, a full view of the software development process from task/user story definition, through to the ultimate delivery to the end customer. A key feature of Kanban is about limiting the amount of work in progress at any one time to not swamp anyone on the team.

A key term here was Work in Progress. Let's dig into this a bit further.

Work in Progress

Work in progress (or WIP for short) limiting lets you define the maximum amount of work that should appear in each state of your software production workflow. The idea behind limiting the amount of work in progress is that these limits help you improve the throughput of work through the system and enables you to get those items to work to "Done" faster. By "Done," we mean delivered into production, so your customers can start using the features.

During development, it's straightforward to think that you can pause working on one task while you make a start on another task. Having two tasks in progress at a time for a developer means that person needs to context switch between two different tasks, or transfer work to other teammates.

Ramping down on one task, and ramping up on another isn't free of effort, it takes time and degrades focus and potentially quality. It's always better to work through the original task entirely first rather than starting, and not completing new tasks. In other words, work in progress limits discourages us from impeding our flow by switching between tasks.

To Do	In Progress	Code Review	QA	Done

A typical Kanban board layout

When working with Kanban, the team will have either a physical Kanban board or an electronic Kanban board. This board is split into different columns. These columns can be different between teams, but essentially you have something like you can see above with a "To Do," "In Progress," "Code Review," "QA" and "Done" column.

When using a board like this, the team should make a decision together to determine the work in progress limits for each status column. The board doesn't have to be limited to these columns. The columns above are an example; you can have whatever state that makes sense to your team. For example, in between the "QA" and "Done" column, you may have a "Ready for Release" if you batch your releases up to once a week.

To Do (2)	In Progress (4)	Code Review (3)	QA (3)	Done

Kanban board with Work in Progress limits set

On the example board above, work in progress limits has been set on four statuses: "To Do," "In Progress," "Code Review" and "QA." As there is nothing left to do once an issue reaches the "Done" column, there is no need for a work in progress limit there. The "To Do" column signifies that the user story has been approved by the product owner and team ready for development. The development team then pulls work from "To Do" column into "In Progress" column as they start to work on user stories. As a good practice, it's wise to keep enough work in the "To Do" column so that each member of the development team can remain fully utilized. By keeping just enough user stories in the "To Do" column, the product owner doesn't become too far ahead of the rest of the team when it comes to defining and setting requirements, and the team becomes more responsive to change.

The "In Progress" column lists work that's under active development by the team. The goal of work in progress limits, in this case, is to ensure that everyone on the team has work to do, but no one is multitasking.

On the board in the following diagram, the limit for "In Progress" items are 4, and there are currently three items in that column. This tells the team they've got the extra capacity to take on more user story/or work item. As a good practice, some development teams set the maximum work in progress limit below the number of team members. The idea is to allow room for following good agile practices like TDD. If a developer finishes an item, but the team is already at their work in progress limit, they know it's time to help assist with a few code reviews or join another developer for some pair programming.

To Do (2)	In Progress (4)	Code Review (3)	QA (3)	Done
Task	Task	Task	Task	Task
Task	Task	Task		
	Task	Task		

The code review column is at full capacity

The "Code Review" column indicates stories that have been fully developed but need to be code reviewed by other members of the development team before being merged back into the main code base. Timely code reviews are a good practice that helps to maintain the overall quality of your codebase, get innovative ideas out to market faster, and spread knowledge across the development team. Items in this state should be acted on urgently.

Planning, Cycle Time, and Focus

A team practicing Kanban is mostly focused on work that is actively in progress. Once a work item has been completed, the team takes the next item out of the "To Do" column. A team's product owner can re-arrange and re-prioritize work in the "To Do" column without affecting the team as they only take items from this column when they have completed what they are currently working on. Team members should always take their next item off the top of the "To Do" column which is why the product owner should always ensure this column is ranked in order of value to the customer.

Minimizing cycle time

As with our discussions in this book on value stream mapping, the cycle time is an important metric for teams using Kanban. As with value stream mapping, the cycle time is the amount of time it takes for an item of work to go through the team's workflow from inception to delivery. By keeping an eye on and optimizing this cycle time a team can more easily forecast the delivery of future work.

Overlapping skill sets from cross-functional development teams leads to smaller cycle times. When only one person holds a skill set, that person becomes a bottleneck in the workflow. This is also true if team members are in silos in particular areas of a system. Teams employ basic best practices like code reviewing and mentoring to help to spread knowledge. Shared skills mean that team members can take on lots of different types of work, which helps to optimize the cycle time of items moving across the board. This also means that if any of the columns get blocked, people on the team are crossed skilled enough to be able to help out and unblock the column.

In a Kanban framework, it's the entire team's responsibility to ensure work is moving smoothly through the process.

Visualize work

Kanban creates a visual model of work flowing through the board. Making the work visible, along with blockers, bottlenecks, and queues, instantly lead to increased communication and collaboration on the development team. This is where either the physical Kanban board or an electronic Kanban comes in. Electronic Kanban systems are great if everyone has them on their screen all the time, or on a large team monitor, but I must admit that there is nothing quite like a giant physical board partitioned into columns with post-it notes being stuck on them.

Scrum vs Kanban

Scrum and Kanban are two different techniques that have an emphasis on productivity, quality and efficiency for business. A common question though, is should I use Scrum or Kanban? It is a fair question, but a better question might be what parts of both methodologies can you efficiently use to develop your software products or services.

We have looked at both approaches, and it should be up to the development and customer product teams to choose what framework will work best for them. Kanban and scrum both share some similar concepts but they both have very different approaches. You should not confuse with the another.

	Scrum	Kanban
Cadence	Fixed sprints (i.e. 2 weeks)	Continuous flow
Release Method	At the end of the sprint	Continuous delivery
Roles	Product owner, scrum master, development team	No existing roles
Key Metrics	Velocity	Cycle time
Change	Strive to not make changes mid sprint	Change can happen at any time

Scrum vs Kanban

First, when we look at the cadence, Scrum works typically in fixed size sprints, usually two weeks in length but this can vary. Kanban, on the other hand, doesn't slice work into sprints. It uses a continuous flow of work where work comes into the "To Do" column and flows through each other state in the workflow without violating the work in progress limits that have been set for each column

Next, we have the Release methodology. In Scrum, you try to deploy a working system at the end of each sprint if approved by the product owner and business. With Kanban, you practice continuous delivery of software into production at the team's discretion, which is why having a robust continuous integration and delivery pipeline setup is so important no matter whether you are following Scrum, Lean or Kanban.

The next difference is that of roles in the team. With Scrum, you have set roles like the Scrum master, product owner, and development team. With Kanban, you don't have any fixed roles; everyone is a member of the team.

The next main difference is that of key metrics. With Scrum, the main metric you care about is the velocity. Velocity is a measure of the amount of work a team can tackle during a single Sprint. Velocity is calculated at the end of the team's sprint by totalling the Points for all fully completed User Stories. For Kanban, the main metric you care about is the cycle time. This is the time it takes for a task to be developed, code reviewed, tested and deployed into the hands of the user. If you remember back to our look at value stream mapping in earlier chapters, we also talked about cycle time as the time it took a request to go through the entire value stream and bring benefit to the end user.

The final difference to look at is that there is a difference in change philosophy. With Scrum, teams should strive not to make changes to the sprint forecast during the sprint. Doing so compromises their learnings around estimation. In Kanban, though changes can happen at any time as there is no fixed sprint but a continuous flow of work.

Some teams like to blend the ideal of Kanban and scrum into a hybrid methodology called Scrumban. Scrumban is where you take the fixed length sprints (such as two-week sprints) and the roles from Scrum such as scrum master, product owner, etc., and the focus on work in progress limits and cycle time from Kanban. With new teams just starting out with agile, it is probably better to choose one methodology or the other and run with it for a while.

Summary

In this book, we first looked at the more traditional Waterfall and V-Model development methodologies and discussed how they don't work very well for modern large-scale projects due to the big bang nature of deployments.

We then looked at the agile development philosophy and how it focuses on delivering value to the customer in smaller increments.

Agile covers four main guiding values, and these values are what the different agile software development practices are base

These values are:

- Individuals and interactions over processes and tools
- Working software over comprehensive documentation
- Customer collaboration over contract negotiation
- Responding to change over following a plan

Next, we took a detailed look at the Extreme Programming development methodology.

Extreme Programming is an engineering-based discipline that contains many rules that need to be followed. Extreme Programming is a useful framework, but teams can be put off by its initial complexity to follow all the rules and can be difficult to follow for a team that is trying to transition into agile from the waterfall.

Scrum, on the other hand, is a more lightweight project management framework that doesn't contain any engineering practices. What is quite common is for a team to adopt scrum to it more lightweight nature and then pick various engineering disciples from extreme programming that suit the team like Test Driven Development and Continuous integration.

When then started looking at Lean Manufacturing and Lean Software Development. I hope you have found it interesting and inspired to try and practice some of its principles in your organizations. To recap, here are the main principles of Lean.

- Eliminate Waste

- Amplify Learning

- Decide as Late as Possible

- Deliver as Fast as Possible

- Empower the Team

- Build Quality / Integrity in?

- See the Whole

This book has been designed to give you a reasonably high-level look at Lean with enough information for you to start applying its principles. Lean is a very deep subject that can go into a lot of detail. If you are interested in learning more, then I recommend some other books by Mary and Tom Poppendiecks.

  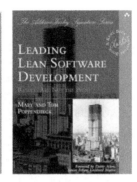

Further reading

These are:

- Lean software development: an agile toolkit.

- Implementing lean software development

- And Leading lean software development

Each of these books is excellent and they go into extreme detail with lots of case studies.

Thanks for reading.

Thank you for purchasing, A Gentle Introduction to Speaking in Public. If you like this book, I would be very grateful for you leaving a review on Amazon. I read all reviews and will try to address any constructive feedback with updates to the book. You can review the book in your country at the following links, or from your local Amazon website.

Amazon.com

Amazon.co.uk

Amazon.de

Amazon.fr

If you enjoyed this book, you might like other books I have in the "Gentle Introduction To" series. I have written these short guides to focus on specific niches and make them brief enough to read in a short space of time, but also detailed enough that they offer a lot of value.

If you wish to see what other high-value books I have in this series, then please visit my web page at the following link.

https://stephenhaunts.com/books/

23461198R00114

Made in the USA
Columbia, SC
08 August 2018